A GUIDE TO GREAT
GRANDPARENTING

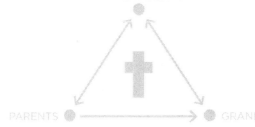

A GUIDE TO GREAT GRANDPARENTING

The God-Given and God-Driven Family Trinity

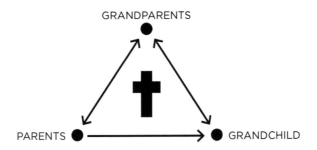

GRANDPARENTS

PARENTS → GRANDCHILD

Paul and Diana Miller

CHRISTIAN
GRANDPARENTNG
NETWORK
CHRISTIANGRANDPARENTING.NET

Who Should Read This Book?

Expectant grandparents-to-be

People who are about to become new grandparents can learn from this book about the great changes that are coming to their lives and prepare them for new relationships, roles, and responsibilities. What lies ahead is not exactly what most people expect or are led to believe. In fact, grandparenting is as much about your relationship with your adult children as it is about your grandchildren. Those who focus only on the grandkids will miss out on the joy of helping and being with their adult children.

Grandparents who want to get better

We think grandparenting is best done in the context of the "God-Given and God Driven Family Trinity" that consists of three generations (grandparents, parents, and grandchildren) and the unique relationships that exist among them. This book shows that grandparents can help most by coaching their adult children, which means replacing their old parent-child relationship with a new and improved version. Specifically, the adult children's newly-experienced ability to love their child unconditionally triggers new-found respect and love for the grandparents that can change everything for the better!

Grandparents who aren't sure what to do

This book also guides grandparents who are uncertain about their roles and responsibilities. How much should they be involved? When should they stand back and watch? What's the difference between helping and interfering? What should they do about babysitting, spoiling, and gift-giving? The answers are different from what many think and what a lot of books say. We think this guidance will liberate and empower grandparents to build better relationships in their Family Trinity.

Grandparents in special situations

Have you become a grandparent by adoption? Have your adult children decided to get involved in foster care? Does your growing family include new members who come from different cultures? This book will help you learn what these situations involve and get insight into how you can contribute as only grandparents can!

Grandparents in difficult situations

Has your family felt the pain and difficulties that come from such things as death, divorce, disability, detachment, and deployment? These situations surely call on grandparents to step up to new roles and responsibilities. This book explains how to do your part to help sustain the family's stability and courageously get through these struggles.

What Others Have Said

"Very few sources lay out the multi-generational responsibilities in a family structure, and even fewer that do it from a Christian perspective. Paul and Diana Miller have not only defined those responsibilities in this book, they have lived them out in their family. Grandparents will read this book and say, 'I wish I had known this when I was younger,' because it is just full of great stuff. It moves from a great visual structure for proper family relationships to wonderful, wise, practical advice for functioning well as a multi-generational family. I'm not aware of another book like this one; I promise you that following its principles will do wonders for your family's relationships!"

LARRY FOWLER
Chief Executive Officer, The Legacy Coalition

"A second path to becoming great grandparents is by carrying out our grandparent role in such a way that brings the best out of our children and grandchildren. Paul and Diana Miller have turned this concept into a doable strategy, which is why we're glad you picked up this book. When you're done reading it, you're going to be glad you did too … and your extended family is going to be much better off because you did."

DR. TIM & DARCY KIMMEL
Co-authors of *Extreme Grandparenting: the Ride of Your Life*

For many years we have witnessed the way Paul and Diana Miller have modeled heroic self-sacrifice in parenthood. Now they do the same as grandparents and share insights for all of us called to the God-ordained honor of being someone's Grandpa or Grandma. Read and glean!"

KURT BRUNER, author of *It Starts At Home*
OLIVIA BRUNER, author of *The Minivan Years*

"If you think grandparenting is just about the grandkids, think again. Paul and Diana's carefully crafted concept of the Family Trinity birthed from their experiences as parents and grandparents will bring many "ah-ha" moments for grandparents. If you're serious about being a truly "great" Christian grandparent—one whose legacy will outlive you generation after generation—you must read this book… and share it with your adult children."

CAVIN HARPER

Author of *Courageous Grandparenting*
Founder and Executive Director, Christian Grandparenting Network

"Paul and Diana add a fresh and practical perspective for grandparenting. Their guidance has been timely for helping us learn to coach our adult children and understand more about our role in this journey of raising the next generation."

KEVIN AND KATIE DIFELICE
Grandparents

"By clearly defining the role of grandparent coach, Paul and Diana have helped me stop trying to be a "father-corrector" and given me deeper enjoyment in relating to my adult children and grandchildren. I am now learning better ways to observe character, listen, give value, and pray unceasingly in the midst of the fun and confusion. The Millers' fresh-air insights have blown away pressure generated by the myth that I had to ensure my grandchildren grew up the "right" way. Now I know that what I need to do most is bless my family, often by just being there cheering from the sidelines."

DR. GARY JEWELL
Grandfather and Family Physician

Table of Contents

Foreword

Dr. Tim & Darcy Kimmel
Co-authors of *Extreme Grandparenting: the Ride of Your Life*

There are two ways to become great grandparents. The first way is the one that's been around since Adam and Eve's grandchildren had kids of their own. It's one of those default titles we get to use if we happen to live long enough to watch our grandchildren become parents.

A second path to becoming great grandparents is by carrying out our grandparent role in such a way that brings the best out of our children and grandchildren. This is an *earned* title. Notice that we listed our *children* in the equation. Once they have children of their own, our role in their lives takes on a critical new dimension that calls for some deliberate dynamics on our part as their parents.

There's a grand myth out there that too many grandparents embrace. It's the myopic assumption that the role of grandparent is played out between two entities—the grandparent and the grandchild. This misses the point of grandparenting by light years. It's a toxic plan that not only does enormous harm to the parents involved, but also to the grandchildren we're called to love.

If we want to have this second version of the title "great grandparent" apply to us, we've got to be unselfishly deliberate when it comes to how we both view and interact with our grown children. We not only want to continue to be good parents to them, but also allies and assets to their ability to be good parents to our grandchildren.

Fortunately, we know two people who have turned this concept of "great" grandparenting into a doable strategy for you and me. Paul and Diana Miller unpack this triune relationship between grandparents, their children (including in-law children) and their grandchildren in a way that goes to the core of what grace looks like handed down through three generations.

That's why we're glad you picked up this book. When you're done reading it, you're going to be glad you did too ... and your extended family picture is going to be much better off because you did.

Authors' Preface

Because you're reading this page, you're probably asking: who are these people and why did they write this book? You're also wondering whether anything in these pages can be useful to you.

With regard to that second point, we're certain you'll benefit from what we have to say. We believe that's true because our firsthand experience helped us discover many ideas on how to improve our grandparenting skills. We've also been encouraged by positive comments from others who have studied these concepts. As a result, we're confident you'll have more than a few "Aha!" moments as you go through the book.

So, who are we? To start, we're grandparents of eight grandchildren, six in one family and two in the other. Further, we both knew our own grandparents very well and basked in their love. In addition, our parents were active grandparents to our children. We've also been involved in helping Cavin Harper, founder of the *Christian Grandparenting Network*, first by reviewing his manuscript that became *Courageous Grandparenting*, and then by participating in his GrandCamp© ministry.

As for our professional background, we're both educators. We like to call ourselves the "bookends" because Paul was university faculty for 43 years and Diana taught preschool for 26 years. In addition, Paul has taught Bible classes for older adults since 1989 in our Colorado Springs church, Woodmen Valley Chapel. This privilege has put both of us in the company of many experienced God-following grandparents.

The idea for this book materialized soon after we learned we would become grandparents. As we looked for guidance, we were surprised that virtually every author and advisor we consulted strongly focused on how we grandparents ought to relate to our grandchildren. It was as if our adult children didn't matter. However, we were hungry for help on our relationship with them as well as the grandkids.

If you share that same hunger, or if you, like many others, are eager to learn more about the benefits of supporting and coaching your grandchildren's parents, you'll find this book to be helpful.

Paul and Diana Miller
Colorado Springs

SECTION 1:
Introduction

This section describes the concept of the Family Trinity and its origins, its structure, and its members' responsibilities.

In particular, we explain that the three-generation Trinity offers great advantages for raising up productive and otherwise functional young people. This structure can be found in families in all cultures around the world, although it's not necessarily acknowledged or put into effect.

We're certain that those advantages are most likely to be harvested when this God-given Family Trinity is also God-driven.

CHAPTER 1

Introducing the Family Trinity

Psalms 1:1-3,6 *Blessed is the man who does not walk in the counsel of the wicked or stand in the way of sinners or sit in the seat of mockers. But his delight is in the law of the LORD, and on his law he meditates day and night. He is like a tree planted by streams of water, which yields its fruit in season and whose leaf does not wither. Whatever he does prospers. ... For the LORD watches over the way of the righteous...*

A few days before Thanksgiving, sometime ago, Diana's obstetrician assured her that our first child would not be born for at least another week. So, on Thursday, we enjoyed a traditional and large meal with Paul's sister and her family. That night, of course, labor started, just as we were both drifting off. Naturally, sleep wouldn't come. Around 6 AM, we headed to the hospital in an early-season snowfall. It was a long 12 hours before our son, David, was born.

His birth was a shock to him, of course, and a staggering event for us, despite much preparation and anticipation. All the reading and training had not touched on a great surprise for us both. We knew we would be ready to love David with all our hearts. What we hadn't anticipated was that we suddenly loved our own Moms and Dads much more deeply than ever before.

God had blessed us far beyond anything we ever imagined.

This chapter describes the *Family Trinity*, a multigenerational structure that helps stabilize and perpetuate families and communities.

Our path to discovering the Trinity was not complicated – as soon as we became grandparents, we realized we were right in the middle of one! It wasn't long before we recognized we had been in one a generation earlier and another one before that, although we didn't think of it as anything special at the time.

In retrospect after more than 12 years of grandparenting, and watching a great many others, we're certain that what we understand about this structure has made us more successful than we would have been without it. That's exactly why we want to help others learn what we've learned and go on to apply the Family Trinity to their own situations.

To explain those ideas, we've chosen the "God-Given and God-Driven Family Trinity" as the central theme for this book and others that may follow.

BUILDING THE FAMILY TRINITY

Specifically, the Family Trinity consists of a three-generation unit built around three different but very complementary relationships. This structure doesn't just pop up into existence but is built over decades, one generation at a time.

At the beginning of our life as a couple, we are the first generation, as represented here:

US

●

When our child arrives, we're given a new person to love and the second generation is created. The one-way arrow in this next diagram symbolizes the sacrificial and grace-based unconditional love for the child, through thick and thin, whatever happens.[1]

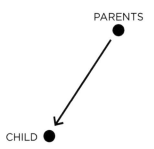

PARENTS

CHILD

Even though our children love us in return, they're not yet able to return to us the same kind of love we feel toward them. However, that situation radically changes when our adult offspring has a child and gives us our grandchild:

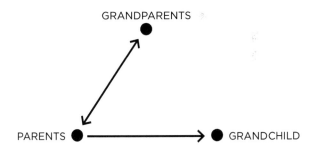

GRANDPARENTS

PARENTS   GRANDCHILD

The one-way arrow at the bottom represents the fact that the new parents love their child unconditionally, just as we sacrificially loved them when they were children.

Perhaps you noticed the changed arrow between the new parents and the grandparents. It now goes *both* ways to represent the parents' new-found and compelling ability to return grace-filled love that flows back to the grandparents. Along with it, the adult children now have a deeper honor and appreciation for what their parents did for them. The end result is a greatly enhanced ability to communicate.

To explain more about this transformation, we know it happens because we personally experienced it. We've also had many others tell us they had the same thing happen to them. Even though we accurately expected our first child's birth to give us a new person to love, we didn't anticipate that it would enable us to love our parents more deeply. Thankfully, we gained a new understanding of how much they had been loving us!

Apparently, we just couldn't fully appreciate our parents' love until we started giving the same love to our newborn son. The exciting result was a new unconditional love for our moms and dads along with more respect and gratitude. In the same way, the birth of our adult children's own first child should allow them and us to enjoy a new relationship. Unlike our previous parent-child relationship, this one is more open because it's built on our shared adult-level experiences and fellowship.

Finally, the diagram of the Family Trinity is completed by adding a two-way arrow between the grandparents and the grandchild:

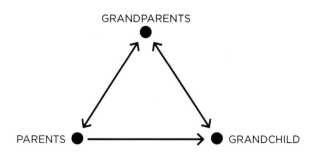

This arrow goes both ways because grandparents and grandchildren innately love each other unconditionally and graciously. That is, neither party has to do, buy, give, or achieve anything to earn that love. It's God's great gift to both generations, and what a blessing it is!

Now, come see what there is to becoming Great Grandparents!

---

1 We acknowledge that no earthly parents can achieve truly unconditional love equivalent to the *agape* love God lavishes on us, his children. However, compared to other relationships, we think it's appropriate to refer to parents' love for their children as unconditional.

CHAPTER 2

The Family Trinity and "Great Grandparenting"

2 Timothy 1:5 *I have been reminded of your sincere faith, which first lived in your grandmother Lois and in your mother Eunice and, I am persuaded, now lives in you also.*

In the first century, a young man named Timothy grew up in what is now southern Turkey. From Paul's words quoted above, it's clear he had been raised in a Family Trinity that consisted of at least his mother and grandmother.

Although we know nothing of his grandfather or whether his Greek father was a Christ-follower, we can be certain that Timothy grew up in a multigenerational household where he was loved, nurtured, and otherwise prepared to be Paul's companion and disciple as well as a significant leader in the early church.

The results of his family's efforts are reflected throughout the New Testament in Paul's descriptions of Timothy as his "fellow-worker" (Romans 16:21), his "brother" (1 Thessalonians 3:2), "my true son, in the faith" (1 Timothy 1:2) and, most affectionately, "my son, whom I love" (1 Corinthians 4:17).

Even though no one knows exactly what Lois did, Paul's praise shows that she must have been a "Great Grandparent"!

Most everything in this book reflects the Family Trinity. That's true simply because what we call "Great Grandparenting" involves living and loving within two new multigenerational relationships with both our grandchildren and their parents. How wonderful it is to have the joy of receiving new, rich love from two directions, and giving it back!

As a result, we've been first puzzled and then frustrated as our culture mistakenly focuses on grandparents' love for the grandchildren without describing this beautiful new relationship with the parents. For some reason, we find that most authors of grandparenting books prescribe how grandparents should relate to their grandchildren without describing this other new family bond.

As a result, we're happy to proclaim that *Great Grandparenting is not just about the grandchildren!*

RESPONSIBILITIES IN THE FAMILY TRINITY

We find the Family Trinity concept to be especially useful because it helps us understand which responsibilities and roles go with each of the three relationships.

Of course, we fully realize that reality is more complex than any diagram can show. However, we suggest that this version can help everyone understand the different responsibilities for grandparents and parents:

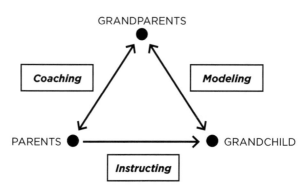

To begin, our first responsible role as grandparents is to *coach our adult children* as they learn how to parent. We support this idea because coaches stay on the sidelines and encourage those who are playing the game. In addition, coaches can help rookies improve because they now know a lot more than they did when they were players themselves. We also note that good coaches only suggest what players can do without demanding or expecting perfect compliance. This behavior reflects the coach's respect for the player as a separate responsible individual with independent decision-making ability. Finally, we point out that coaches don't run out onto the field to push aside the players and take their place in the game!

With regard to the parents' first responsibility, we find that it is *instructing their children*. It's crucial that this role be respected by grandparents who want to create a healthy Family Trinity. It's also crucial that wise parents not abdicate their instructing responsibility to the grandparents. However, they may choose to welcome appropriate coaching and empower the grandparents to help them learn how to be good fathers and mothers.

Grandparents also have a special responsibility to help their grandchildren grow up well. As we see it, they are to *model appropriate behavior for the grandchildren*. This modeling teaches by demonstrating instead of lecturing or testing. Importantly, modeling means that grandparents have to be on their toes at all times because children learn just as much or more by watching as being taught directly.

To be perfectly clear, we strongly believe that grandparents should not feel or behave as if they are instructors of the grandchildren on equal footing with the parents. The only exception is when they are compelled to take over because of difficult circumstances that take the parents out of the picture.

HOW MANY GENERATIONS?
There's a big point that we think should motivate grandparents to be good models for their grandchildren. Specifically, we've observed that most people tend to mimic their parents when they're parenting but

tend to mimic their grandparents when they're grandparenting.

Because that's so, the grandparenting behavior we model to our grandchildren is likely to be duplicated by them when they're grandparents to our great-great-grandchildren, some four generations after us. Further, our great-great-grandchildren's behavior can eventually affect the behavior and attitudes of *their* grandchildren, who will be our great-great-great-great-grandchildren!

This diagram shows how what grandparents do (or don't do) can impact four and even six generations of descendants.

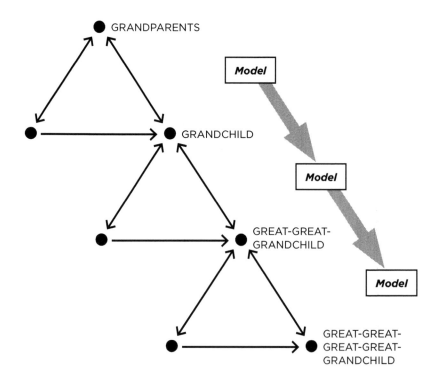

EVERY FAMILY TRINITY IS DIFFERENT

This multigenerational diagram suggests another valuable point.

Specifically, early in our married life, the two of us were part of a Family Trinity involving our grandparents and parents. When we later began parenting our children and our parents became their grandparents, we helped create another Family Trinity. When our children had children, we then again assumed a different role in yet another Family Trinity. Each one is similar but different. That outcome is only to be expected for a multitude of reasons, even though each one will be shaped by what went on before.

Therefore, grandparents must never doubt the power and ability of preceding generations to impact those that follow for many, many years. At issue for each generation is whether that impact will be *positive* or *negative*. It almost goes without saying that grandparents can have a powerful impact on which direction it goes.

MAINTAINING STABILITY

One way that grandparents can help pass down positive values is to help maintain a stable Family Trinity. A key factor for stability is consistently honoring the three general responsibilities of coaching, instructing, and modeling. Each generation should carefully operate within those boundaries so that these two negative outcomes don't occur:

- When grandparents continue instructing their adult children instead of making the transition to coaching them, they're sending the signal that they've not yet relinquished their parents' role. For one thing, this failure to release the adult children can dysfunctionally prolong their maturing process. It can also cause friction after they become parents because they will surely resent any unwelcome meddling by the grandparents.

- When grandparents directly instruct their grandchildren instead of modeling suitable good behavior for them, friction and instability will surely follow. First, the youngsters will be easily confused when their grandparents and parents teach them different things. Second, it will cause the parents to resent the grandparents' encroachment on their responsibility.

To be clear, grandparents have many perfectly good ways to engage in teaching activities with their grandchildren that should not create issues. For example, they can occasionally tell family stories, explain traditions, do crafts to develop rapport, or just hang out together and enjoy each other's company. Special moments can emerge when they teach certain skills to the grandkids, like cooking, sewing, fishing, gardening, playing golf, or the like without infringing on the parents' responsibilities.

DEALING WITH INSTABILITY

Because of the world's broken nature, a Family Trinity may lack stability through tragic and unfortunate circumstances. However, even in bad situations, stability can be restored by shifting, sharing, and otherwise reassigning the key responsibilities.

In particular, grandparents may have to begin instructing the grandchildren if the parents are temporarily or permanently unable to do it. While this arrangement differs from the ideal, the grandparents' patience and love can produce spectacular results. (More guidance on these situations appears in the third and fourth sections of this book.)

WHY THE FAMILY TRINITY MATTERS

So, there you have it: the Family Trinity is ideally a set of three healthy relationships that should create a stable three-generation family and set the stage for many more generations to come. However, life is seldom, if ever, ideal!

Instead, it's virtually certain that every family has some damage because of what we call the "D" factors: death, disability, deployment, detachment, dysfunction, and divorce. Even in these stressful situations, the grandparents' and parents' knowledge of the Family Trinity with its roles and responsibilities can help a family adapt and survive.

In fact, multigenerational stability makes it easier to get things back on track for the benefit of the present Family Trinity and later ones yet to come.

THERE'S MORE TO IT

Now, as Christians, we're very willing to acknowledge that God is the architect of the Family Trinity. It's such a beautiful arrangement that it just has to be GOD-GIVEN! No one should be surprised that this structure can be found in all families in all cultures.

Beyond that point, we cannot conceive how it can ever work as well as it's designed to work unless the Holy Spirit is acting as the *powerful gravity* in the center, holding it all together while touching each member with God's grace just as they need to be touched. Thus, our aim for our family, and for yours, is that the Family Trinity will reach its full potential by being both GOD-GIVEN AND GOD-DRIVEN.

Further, we know that this outcome can be achieved by putting Christ in the center, touching everyone and shaping their actions and, indeed, their lives. This version of the diagram illustrates what we mean:

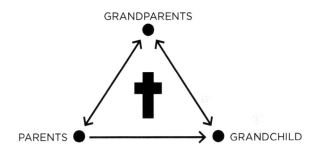

CHAPTER 3

The Grandparent's First Role

Deuteronomy 6:1-2 *These are the commands, decrees and laws the LORD your God directed me to teach you to observe in the land that you are crossing the Jordan to possess, so that* **you, your children and their children after them** *may fear the LORD your God as long as you live by keeping all his decrees and commands that I give you, and so that you may enjoy long life.*

Deuteronomy 4:8-9 *And what other nation [beside Israel] is so great as to have such righteous decrees and laws as this body of laws I am setting before you today? Only be careful, and watch yourselves closely so that you do not forget the things your eyes have seen or let them slip from your heart as long as you live. Teach them [and make them known]* **to your children and to their children after them.**

When we started sharing the news with friends that our son, Greg, and his wife, Christine, would soon be having their first child and our first grandchild, many friends commented: "Oh, it's going to be so much fun being around those grandchildren." The next most frequent was: "I just know you're going to love baby-sitting the grandkids." The one that grated our nerves the most was: "It'll be wonderful spoiling those kids and sending them home!"

Our family's own history is reflected in this chapter. When we were expectant grandparents, we encountered two thoughts. As described in the story, we experienced a very strong *external* sense that everyone was expecting us to be excited only about what we could do with and for our grandchildren.

In contrast, we had a stronger *internal* sense that we wanted to be positive grandparents who would help our children and their children build solid families.

While we were definitely eager about the grandchildren, we were just as pleased about seeing our offspring and their spouses become parents so we could enjoy a greatly enhanced and deeper relationship with them. Twelve years and eight grandchildren later, we've learned that this attitude has magnified our ability to positively influence our family.

FIRST THING FIRST

When we combine all our experiences and weigh what they mean, we keep coming back to this fundamental idea that makes Great Grandparenting possible: *The first role for grandparents is supporting the parents of the grandchildren in raising them to love God and follow Christ.*

This idea is based on the premise that the grandparents' first essential task in the Family Trinity is to be the *coach* for the parents of their grandchildren. That premise makes it clear that grandparents are to avoid (1) directly instructing their adult children about parenting and (2) encroaching on the parents' own responsibility for directly instructing the grandchildren.

IT ISN'T JUST ABOUT THE GRANDCHILDREN

To paraphrase H.L. Mencken, a prominent social critic from a century ago, there are "easy" solutions to difficult challenges that seem completely natural, easy, and totally feasible, yet they most often turn out to be totally wrong. And, so it is with grandparenting!

Our friends were unwittingly offering easy ideas about our daunting new role as grandparents – nothing but fun, fun, fun without any responsibility. While it's possible to approach this status with that light-hearted attitude, the real task is more challenging, but, oh so much more satisfying and long-lasting.

As a result, we expect the most startling idea in this book for most people is the one we introduced in Chapter 2: *grandparenting isn't just about our grandchildren*. While our grandkids are doubtlessly very special and precious, we grandparents have relationships with their parents, our adult children, that are just as special.

COACHING EXPLAINED

In fulfilling our coaching responsibility, our main jobs are to be a support, a help, a backup, a guide, a fellow-traveler, a prayer partner, and an encourager for the parents while they raise up their children. To put it another way, we grandparents ought to pursue the objective expressed in the sixth chapter of Deuteronomy: helping our children's children eventually become all they can and should be – healthy, happy, loving, productive, generous, God-loving and Christ-following adults.

The final word in the previous sentence might be a shock or a wake-up call for many people. When you see your new little grandbaby, the last thing you're inclined to think of is their adulthood and their own children. But, if you realize how quickly the time passed between your child's birth and their parenthood, WOW!

In other words, this grandparenting obligation to help the parents produce responsible adults is completely real and incredibly urgent.

A LONG-TERM INVESTMENT

In addition, when we get a vision for our grandchildren as adults, we should realize that we're making investments that are so long term that we may never see the results.

Sure, depending on longevity and the parents' age when their children are born, some, but not all, of us will actually see and hold our great-grandchildren. Nonetheless, it's likely that our family will eventually include great- and great-great-grandchildren. Even if we aren't around when they arrive and grow up, what we accomplish as models for our grandchildren can still impact those descendants, so we should surely remain diligent coaches as long as we can.

Such was the case for the Israelites when Moses issued God's instructions to them in Deuteronomy 6. Specifically, it is His desire that His people's vision of the future must not selfishly ignore the many more days, years, and generations that will come to pass long after they've died. (We happily point out that Deuteronomy 6 describes a Family Trinity consisting of "you, your children and their children after them.")

Regardless of whether we'll get to see the outcome of this process with our own earthly eyes, our goal should be just the same – obedience to God's command that we strive to be Great Grandparents.

CONFRONTING REALITY

Surely, not every family gets to live the conceptual ideal life suggested by the Family Trinity's structure. In fact, each family has or will have something out of the ordinary because of unusual and tragic situations: a deceased grandparent, an absent parent, blended families with step-grandchildren (a term we prefer to avoid using), broken relationships, and so forth. While it's still out of the ordinary, more and more grandparents are taking on the main care-giving roles for their grandchildren.

In all these tough cases, the fact remains that the first role and responsibility of grandparenting is to support the parents in raising up grandchildren to become productive and well-adjusted adults. Nothing fully excuses grandparents for not trying to help and encourage the parents, although

DIGGING INTO THE WORD!

At the beginning of this chapter, we quoted another key verse that can guide grandparents. It is Deuteronomy 4:9, in which the New International Version, among others, translates the Hebrew word "yadah" as "teach" when it says: "Only be careful, and watch yourselves closely so that you do not forget the things your eyes have seen or let them slip from your heart as long as you live. Teach them [and make them known] to your children and to their children after them." This interpretation certainly supports our understanding that grandparents have the essential roles of "coaching" and "modeling" succeeding generations.

We inserted *"and make them known"* in addition to *"teach"* to convey a likely broader meaning of "yadah." For example, the English Standard Version also uses that phrase.

We actually prefer "make them known" because it clarifies that grandparents can obey this command by filling their first role of helping their adult children obey their own command to pass the full knowledge of and faith in God's great goodness on to their children.

In addition, the context makes it clear that the command from Moses applies to the whole nation of Israel. As a result, we find that "make them known" also charges grandparents with the responsibility to not only coach and model but also to directly instruct their grandchildren if and when the parents are unable or unwilling to meet their responsibility to teach spiritual truth.

there certainly can be obstacles that are difficult or seemingly impossible to overcome. In these tough situations, grandparents have to acknowledge their Biblical responsibility to do what they can to influence their children's children to grow up to be God-loving and Christ-following adults.

Let's turn now to some practical things that we grandparents can do to help our adult children bring up our grandchildren.

SECTION 2:
Some Key Behaviors

Now that we've established the Family Trinity's structure and the responsibilities of its adult members, this section presents our recommendations for key behaviors that will help them work toward the goal of nurturing the grandchildren to become productive and functional new adults.

The specific topics include turning the adult children free to live their lives and become successful parents, the nature of the communication channels in the Trinity, the differences between help and interference, and the importance of reinforcing what the parents are teaching their grandchildren without undermining their efforts.

Please note that the contents of these chapters are often conceptual. As such, they don't apply to every situation that grandparents may encounter. Sections 3 and 4 provide more of that practical advice, but you're more likely to be able to implement those tools after reading the next four chapters.

CHAPTER 4

They May Be Our Children But They're Not Children Any More

1 Corinthians 13:11 *When I was a child, I talked like a child, I thought like a child, I reasoned like a child. When I became a man, I put childish ways behind me.*

We have a friend in her 80's who still worries whether her 55-year old son will ever be a success. We know another couple with a son who has two failed marriages and hasn't been able to hold a good job. Despite the fact that he's middle-aged, they continue to send support checks for car payments and such.

A sadder tale is a grandmother who just keeps butting into her adult child's family life as if she is the resident matriarch, even though she lives many miles away. In her eyes, nothing is done well in the household and she has the unquestioned duty to straighten everyone up.

If these people were to be asked why they behave this way, we're sure all three of them would say something like, "A parent's work and responsibilities are never done!"

Once parents become grandparents (and surely sooner), the Family Trinity teaches that it's past the time when they need to do things like calling to check up on their adult children every day or week and otherwise hover over them. It's even less appropriate for grandparents to expect or demand regular calls from their very busy grown children. Regardless of whether they have kept the family's values or gone in an unwanted direction, the offspring are definitely adults, not children, and should be treated that way.

To be clear, we're definitely not suggesting that grandparents should abandon their adult children and their families. Far from it! Rather, we wholeheartedly believe that relationships between grandparents and their adult children can be productive only when the former realize that their responsibilities don't include fretting over the latter and trying to run their lives.

THEY'RE NOT CHILDREN ANY MORE

The key point for this chapter is that we grandparents should completely understand that *our adult children are not children any more!* If we don't act accordingly, we're virtually ensuring that our relationship with them will not mature.

DIGGING INTO THE WORD!

Although Paul's wisdom is evident throughout his letters, we especially like Chapter 13 of First Corinthians because its words informed us when we were dating and still guide us in our married life.

We quote verse 11 at the beginning of this chapter because it conveys God's instruction to parents to *proactively and methodically* train and otherwise prepare their children to become independent adults. Successfully preparing them for adulthood will make them eager to "put their childish ways behind them." It will also prepare their parents to stop clinging to them as if they're still vulnerable children.

This realization should actually start earlier in life when our not-yet-adult children begin to show signs that they're becoming adults. It's good for both them and us if we can actually begin to turn them loose in age-appropriate (and moral) ways when they're younger. If we do it right, they will begin to learn on their own by making mistakes and by doing good things without our being there to ensure they perform.

In contrast, so-called "Helicopter Parents" don't let go and continue hovering over their children far too long in a way that keeps them from growing up. This hyper-protectiveness creates an unsuitable situation in which sons or daughters are more or less compelled to remain child-like instead of standing on their own feet. One devastating outcome is their conditioned belief that they can always count on their parents to rescue them.

Another bitter result of holding on too long is nervous but needless fretting by grandparents who have assumed responsibility for problems that aren't their own. Ironically, while these grandparents might think they're doing a good thing by trying to protect their adult children, it's almost certain that not letting them go will produce miserable outcomes for at least several generations.

After all, the real satisfaction of having an "empty nest" doesn't come only from freeing up the parents to pursue their own interests. Even more satisfaction comes from having prepared the "young birds" for responsible adulthood and parenthood.

LETTING GO IS HARD TO DO

As we all know, children remain vulnerable in one way or another, even when they're young adults. As creatures of habit, we parents often find it difficult to go "hands off" when we're certain they're going to flounder, flop, and fail on their own. However, we just have to let go to help them put their childhood behind them.

To provide this kind of help, we should generally reach the point where we are in standby mode in their late teens or early twenties. By this time, we should have taken our hands off the wheel of their life and committed to keeping them off until we're asked for advice and help. Even when those requests come, we have to stifle our parental urges to take over and protect them.

When responding to our adult children's requests for help or initiating

ACTION  POINT!

We suggest that the best beginning to advisory conversations with adult children (especially parents of our grandchildren) should probably go something like this: "What do you think you need?" or "What do you think you should do next?" These questions should be followed by a long pause on our part before we jump to the next question of "How do you think we might be able to help you?"

Our very strong recommendation is that it's never a good move to indulge an unkind impulse to say something like, "We told you so!" or "We knew this would happen!", no matter how justifiable we might think it would be. Instead, we should find ways to encourage and stimulate them to perform solid self-assessments to figure out what the problem is, what role they played in creating it, and various alternative solutions.

Ideally, they would come to us for assistance in making decisions by asking us to help them sort through the available options. In reality, however, we may have to coach them through the whole process, especially when they are younger adults.

It should be noted that our approach must be age-appropriate in the sense that adult children up to about 25 years old have a brain that's still developing an adult-strength ability to make sound decisions.[2] As they get older, and especially more experienced in parenting, we will find them easier to work with and well on their way to needing less guidance and affirmation.

a conversation about a problem, we have found a practice that reminds us of our role. Specifically, our experience shows it's far better to ask *gentle questions* than to make declarative statements. We certainly must not end a conversation with strong imperative sentences that tell them what they have to do.

However, we can also tell you it's not always easy to change this behavior!

HANDLING REQUESTS FOR HELP

When adult children become parents, we grandparents can certainly expect new kinds of requests for help to be triggered by the mysteries of parenthood. They are likely to benefit from a lot of our coaching in this stage, but their inexperience at parenting doesn't justify taking control like we used to when they were toddlers.

The special, even beautiful, opportunity for grandparents in this early parental phase is the offspring's two-way emotional transformation that comes with a first child. As we described in the first two chapters, their ability to love their own child unconditionally helps them realize they had been getting such love from us all along and still are. That awakening is priceless because it's an important key to our success in coaching them.

With all that said, grandparents still face the question of just what they should do and say in any particular case when their adult children ask for help.

There is no blanket answer that will cover every situation. However, we're confident that grandparents' responses should not be characterized as a rescue from a poor decision's consequences. Even when there are clear needs to respond and extend a hand, adult children will always be better off if they take responsibility for extracting themselves from their situation. Contrary to what we did when they were literally children, it's our new duty to let them feel a pinch, say, even if we could easily bail them out.

Surely, our new responsibility to *not act* will occasionally make us cringe just like we did when they started kindergarten or first rode a bike without training wheels!

Through it all, we must show respect, interest in their situation, patience in listening, and then (the hard part) speaking and acting with wisdom. Remember, we are the coach, not an active player in their game.

ROLE REVERSAL

We can tell you that you will be highly blessed when you see your adult kids actually (and thoroughly) put their childish ways behind them.

One blessing that you can enjoy is knowing you can feel free to ask them for their advice on how to deal with your problems and decisions. We offer more guidance on this point in the next chapter.

---

2 The Massachusetts Institute of Technology has an ongoing effort called the *Young Adult Development Project*. We find this summary to be helpful: "According to recent findings, the human brain does not reach full maturity until at least the mid-20s. The specific changes that follow young adulthood are not yet well studied, but it is known that they involve increased myelination and continued adding and pruning of neurons. As a number of researchers have put it, 'the rental car companies have it right.' The brain isn't fully mature at 16, when we are allowed to drive, or at 18, when we are allowed to vote, or at 21, when we are allowed to drink, but closer to 25, when we are allowed to rent a car." hrweb.mit.edu/worklife/ youngadult/brain.html (Accessed January 2017)

CHAPTER 5

Communication, Communication, Communication!

Ephesians 4:2 *Be completely humble and gentle; be patient, bearing with one another in love.*

Ephesians 4:15 *… speaking the truth in love, we will in all things grow up into him who is the Head, that is, Christ.*

Ephesians 4:29 *Do not let any unwholesome talk come out of your mouths, but only what is helpful for building others up according to their needs, that it may benefit those who listen.*

Even though it happened in 2003, I [Paul] wistfully remember my last visit with my Dad about six weeks before he died at age 89. I had set up the plane trip to Houston and reserved a rental car and a hotel room. When I called to tell him my plans, he insisted that I use a taxi to get to his house, which he had temporarily vacated to go into a rehab facility, and then drive his car. Even though doing so meant inconvenience and sleeping in the same room I occupied as a 4-year old, I did as he wished. After all, he was my father.

When I got to the facility, he didn't invite me in for a chat but followed his greeting with an instruction to "Take me to the barber shop!" Along the way, he told me to get in one specific lane or another and forcefully chided me that I hadn't signaled a lane change, didn't turn on the wipers when it started to rain, and didn't turn them off when it quit. Keep in mind that I was 57 years old and a tenured full professor!

Throughout my visit, we mostly talked about his issues. My deep concern for his deteriorating situation was accompanied by my profound regret that we were not in an adult-to-adult relationship.

Looking back on that episode, I realize my father was distracted at the time by his own concerns as a widower nearing the end of his life. Yet, he was acting as if he were the patriarch of a family that had no other responsible and highly functioning adults. As a result, our ability to communicate was hindered. Nonetheless, what happened taught me a valuable lesson.

What the two of us (Paul and Diana) like to say is that the three most crucial keys to successful grandparenting are "Communication, communication, communication." It's no coincidence that the Family Trinity includes three communication channels between grandparent and parent, parent and grandchild, and grandchild and grandparent.

Specifically, if adults want to be wise grandparents in their old age, they will find value in taking early proactive positive steps to develop adult-level communication with their children. They will also benefit from developing skills for communicating with their grandchildren.

RESPONDING TO REQUESTS FOR HELP

We're coming back to the first communication channel between the grandparents and the adult children to explain some more key points. Although that channel has existed between them for years, it should be greatly enhanced when new parents comprehend they have been loved all their lives with the same sort of intense and parental love they now feel toward their own children.

Our advice for improving grandparent-parent communication has two parts. If you already have a good adult-level relationship with the new parents, we encourage you to talk about this new love with them, and openly commit to building an even stronger relationship. On the other hand, if your relationship is not as good as it might be, we urge you to invite the new parents to join you in rebuilding it in light of their revelation. If repentance and forgiveness are needed, give them freely. There is too much at stake here to be stubborn and self-centered. Let this time be the opportunity to lay a solid foundation for the new Family Trinity's future. It's just wonderful when everyone can bask in the peace and joy that can be built on their newly conscious unconditional love for us.

However the situation plays out, this abundance of God-given love should facilitate new open and deep communication between generations. The adult children can ask for guidance and assurance, trusting their parents to be helpful, not dismissive or judgmental. The parents can, in turn, offer help with gentleness and respect for their offspring's maturity and independence.

ACTION  POINT!

To reap the benefits of the grandparent-parent relationship, it's essential that both parties be open and receptive. That means grandparents do well when they first put aside any superior attitude that "We're the only adults here" and then go on to sincerely and fully respect the parents of their grandchildren as equals. The goal should be making them feel comfortable and confident in asking for assistance.

As painful as it might be, it's a great idea for both parties to realize that the younger family will benefit from taking ownership of their problems. This understanding can help them resist the temptation to shirk their responsibilities while giving the grandparents strength to resist the temptation to indulge their conditioned response to take over and fix their problems.

IT GOES BOTH WAYS!

As we grandparents get older, this adult-level and close communication will, or at least should, begin to work in the other direction. In most cases, if we are approaching or already in senior citizen status, we're going to find ourselves needing various kinds of help from our offspring. For some, if not most grandparents, this role reversal is difficult to swallow because they have to admit that they can't make it on their own any more. It's also tough because they're turning for help to the very same people who depended on them when they were both younger.

BECOMING INVISIBLE

With regard to communications between parents and their children, there's one general rule for grandparents: *stay out of the way!*

What grandparents can do is offer gentle help to the parents in dealing with frustrations caused by their kids' behavior, which may include the smiling comment from us, "Oh, it was pretty much like this for us when you were their age…"

ACTION POINT!

Now is a good time to begin involving our adult offspring in our own decisions. We can start with some easy things – like what kind of TV or car to buy, what color carpet might look good, or what they know about computers that would help us. Listen well and follow up on what they say.

Making this kind of shift now will make it easier (but still not easy) when the really tough decisions come up later. Examples are health issues and finances, as well as the infinitely touchy ones of when we should quit driving or move to a smaller place or a senior living center. If we've done things right, they'll be used to being asked and helping and, more importantly, we'll be used to asking and being helped.

Suggestions will probably be welcome, but not in the middle of a heated discussion between the parents and grandchildren. That practice will end up frustrating one party or the other, or even both, especially if it looks like the grandparents are taking sides or just don't understand the issue that's on the table.

Some advice from the grandparents to the parents might be appropriate when the kids aren't around, but it's important to follow the pattern of asking questions, not just giving orders that tell them exactly what they must do.

TALKING TO OUR GRANDCHILDREN

We grandparents can also help smooth things out through our own direct communications with the grandkids. If we've been in their lives, we'll be in their hearts, too. Our presence there can allow our one-on-one chats to be full of impact. It can especially give us a way to bring more gentle love and peace into their communications with their parents.

We can offer other guidance about this communication channel with the grandkids. Specifically, grandparents will do a great work if they will use their chats, emails, and other kinds of interaction to build up the grandchildren's love and respect for their parents. That means respecting what their parents are trying to accomplish with absolutely no undercutting or contradiction.

The grandparents' role of supporting the parents also includes helping strengthen the bridges between them and their kids, not widening that gap. (We have more to say on this advice in the next chapter.)

THE BOTTOM LINE

There's no question that successful communication in the Family Trinity comes about only by doing it God's way with abundant love and patience.

It's also true that good communication brings great joy and satisfaction while also contributing to the grandparents' important mission of helping the parents raise the grandchildren to successful God-loving and Christ-following adulthood.

CHAPTER 6

Your Help is Welcome, Your Interference is Not

James 3:17-18 *But the wisdom that comes from heaven is first of all pure; then peace-loving, considerate, submissive, full of mercy and good fruit, impartial and sincere.*
Peacemakers who sow in peace raise a harvest of righteousness.

Some years ago, Bill, a grandfather we knew, was intensely fixated on the fact that his son and daughter-in-law didn't have an RV for camping with their children. He was upset because his grandkids were going to miss out on the wonderful experiences his family enjoyed while growing up. Even though the son and his wife had explained why they didn't want an RV, Bill bugged them about it, over and over. He also complained to his friends, all of whom knew it wasn't necessary and would cost the family more than they could afford.

For months, every conversation between Bill and his son sooner or later ended up with the question, "When are you going to get an RV?" Even though he phrased it as a question, his son received it as an imperative. Eventually, the son and his wife decided the only peaceful way to bring the interference to an end was to buy an RV, which sits unused in the driveway virtually all the time.

Perhaps the story is an extreme, but we know something like it can happen when grandparents don't recognize the difference between *helping* the younger family and *interfering* with their decisions. In the first case, the motive is passing on wisdom to the next generation. In the second, the motive reflects an inappropriate need to be in control.

HELP

Help happens when grandparents assist their adult children in doing the best they can in raising up the grandchildren. As indicated in this chapter's verse from James 3, heavenly wise help has pure motives, is intended to produce peace, respects the recipients, doesn't have to be accepted, lacks self-interest, produces great results, and has no hidden agendas. The proof that the help is effective is found in the family's peace and righteousness.

If that kind of help happens the right way, the Family Trinity will be stabilized with positive results for generations to come.

INTERFERENCE

On the other hand, *interference* occurs when grandparents think they know how their adult children could be better parents and ungraciously proceed to tell them in unkind ways what they must do. It's even more damaging when they actually say things to the grandchildren that contradict their parents' guidance. These behaviors do nothing but undermine the parents' credibility and authority in their children's eyes.

For example, interference happens when grandparents correct their grandkids before the parents do, usually falling back into a *knee-jerk* response they learned while they were parents. Like any bad habit, it can be defeated with acknowledgement, repentance, and commitment to change; it also may require a bleeding tongue with tooth marks. Whatever it takes, do it!

MANAGING THE CONVERSATION

The temptation to interfere can be especially strong when grandparents are alone with their grandchildren and the kids start moving the conversation toward criticizing their parents. Because their goal could be enlisting help for their side of a conflict with their parents, an effective initial solution may involve graciously turning the discussion to some other topic. If that doesn't succeed, then the grandparent will likely need to lead the grandchildren to understanding how much their parents love them and how they show that love through their actions and attitudes.

By their own experience, all grandparents should realize it's perfectly normal for children to whine and complain about their parents. If you don't think so, dredge up your own childhood memories about how you felt toward your parents' rules and discipline!

We'll assert that it's OK to listen quietly before shushing the grandchildren. Grandparents just have to take the kids' gripes with a grain of salt and a smile. Then, when the children are done and been shown due respect by listening, grandparents should offer up gentle comments to the effect that, "Oh, some day, you'll be happy your parents taught you that lesson" or "I know what you mean because your Mom used to complain to her grandparents about me when she was your age."

TEAMWORK IS BEST
Once upon a time, the two of us heard and immediately rejected this lame joke: "Grandparents and grandchildren are so close because they're united by a common enemy."

ACTION  POINT!

As their grandparents, it's totally out of bounds for us to say critical things to our grandchildren about their parents. That's true when we're responding to the kids' complaints and it's especially more destructive if we bring up our own criticisms. Nothing good can come out of doing that.

To rework an old admonition: "Loose lips sink relation-ships!"

To the contrary, the power of the God-Given and God-Driven Family Trinity shows that grandparents and grandchildren are blessed when they're united by their shared love and respect for God and the parents. That kind of relationship with our grandchildren should be our goal.

NEVER. . .

The advice in this chapter is straightforward: never interfere.

Please notice the period at the end of that sentence. It signifies the absolute nature of that principle of Great Grandparenting.

INTERVENTION

We hate bringing up this point, but interference should not be confused with *intervention*, which must occur if the situation between the parents and grandchildren is so far out of control that it is abusive or dangerously threatening their physical and emotional well-being.

In these most dire circumstances, it's better to leave intervention to the police or social services to avoid making an already bad situation worse. Doing it without their help can endanger everyone, including the grandparents.

We hope and pray that such an extreme difficulty never happens in your family.

CHAPTER 7

Reinforce,
Don't Undermine

Ephesians 6:4 *Fathers, do not exasperate your children; instead,*
bring them up in the training and instruction of the Lord.

We know of a family in which the parents are teaching their children how
to make good choices in their lives. Among their family practices are regular bedtimes, limited television, and little consumption of candy. Because
the parents explained these policies and the children understood them, they
adopted good habits that made their lives more grounded and productive.

One summer, problems began when their grandmother asked to keep the
grandkids for a couple of weeks while the parents enjoyed a nice cruise.
When the youngsters returned home, they wanted to stay up until all
hours, whined to watch lots of mindless TV, and kept raiding the pantry
and fridge looking for sweet treats.

Now, why do you suppose that happened?

This chapter's point is that grandparents should think carefully about *all* their decisions concerning the grandchildren. They will do good to be aligned with the parents' teaching, even if some of it seems a bit unorthodox.

THE FAMILY TRINITY, AGAIN

The remaining link in the Family Trinity is the all-important communication channel between grandchildren and their parents.

It's essential for the parents to set sensible expectations. For one thing, the children's minds are immature and they cannot be held as accountable as adults if they're thinking and acting like kids. For another, they cannot yet understand the nature and depth of their parents' grace-filled unconditional love. As a result, they often take their Mom and Dad for granted. In addition, they aren't going to recognize how much they're cared for, how much their parents do for them, or how many positive qualities their parents have.

In other words, young people don't get it because they can't! They're not psychologically equipped to be aware of the kind of love they're receiving and they're not emotionally capable of returning it anywhere close to the same degree they're receiving it.

Remembering that the Family Trinity connects the grandparents and grandchildren, we suggest that the kids' innate love for the grandparents opens up a channel that can be used to shed useful light on the parents' love for the youngsters.

THE WHOLE FAMILY IS AFFECTED

We now turn to describing the value in recognizing that grandparents' times with their grandchildren are wonderful opportunities to sincerely praise the kids. The grandparents also should praise the parents and *reinforce* the attitudes, behaviors, and values they're trying to instill.

What's especially good about this reinforcing behavior is that it lifts up the whole family.

First, grandchildren will feel good that their own positive qualities and actions have been noticed. Their grandparents' praise will stick like glue, maybe for the rest of their lives.

Second, grandchildren will be more inclined to look on their parents with appreciation after their grandparents sing their praises. Because of the kids' trust in us as their grandparents, our approval for what their parents are doing should penetrate into their hearts and heads.

However, in light of the way that children are emotionally and intellectually "wired," especially teenagers, we cannot expect everything (or even *any*thing) we say to evoke an immediate expressed response that causes them to run to their parents to profusely offer genuine thanks

ACTION  POINT!

When the grandchildren are around, we grandparents should stifle any "suggestions" directed at their parents. We should sit quietly or, if appropriate, speak softly. If we really do have questions and concerns about what's happening in the family, we should wait awhile, and look for a comfortable situation in which we can ask the parents whether we can have their permission to ask some questions and make a suggestion.

If they say "yes," then we can start with praise for what they're doing and then tread carefully. Above all, we shouldn't assert that we know what's best. We should always keep in mind that the way they're raising their family may very well reflect the upbringing of our son's or daughter's spouse. If so, we should wait and see; after all, it might be just as effective as what we did when we were in charge. Or even better!

Finally, once we've made our suggestions, we should move on. If it's a good idea in their eyes, they'll run with it. If it isn't, we did our best.

After all, isn't that what we would have done when we were raising them?

for all they do. Rather, we must keep up the praise consistently over time. If we do, our compliments and reinforcement will bear a rich harvest when our grandchildren go on to raise our great-grandchildren.

THERE'S ENOUGH HONOR TO GO AROUND

God always knows what He is doing, and that's obvious in the fifth commandment when He instructed His people to "Honor your father and your mother so that your days may be long upon the land which the Lord your God is giving you." The Apostle Paul elaborated on this wisdom when he wrote in Ephesians 6 that this instruction "is the first commandment with a promise." We also think it applies in reverse: parents ought to honor their sons and daughters at all times, including when they have become fathers and mothers.

Here's our assurance – *if we grandparents truly honor the parents of our grandchildren, they will honor us even more, and their children will honor them and us more highly, too.*

This, too, is Great Grandparenting.

DIGGING INTO 📖 THE WORD!

The Apostle Paul issued this well-known advice in Ephesians 6:4 "Fathers, do not exasperate your children; instead, bring them up in the training and instruction of the Lord."

Keeping in mind that grandparents are still fathers and mothers to their adult children, and are perhaps finding it hard to let go, we propose this modified paraphrase: "Grandparents, do not exasperate the parents of your grandchildren; instead, help them bring up your grandchildren in the training and instruction of the Lord."

Simply put, if we grandparents aren't helping, we're just getting in the way of some important work!

Some Half-Time Thoughts and Encouragement

At this stage in the book, we hope you have found helpful points for moving ahead in the quest to become "Great Grandparents." We especially hope the Family Trinity has provided insight. Of course, our presentation is incomplete and we've only begun to plumb its depths.

*We have also presented some unconventional guidance for grandparents because our key point is **that the first role for grandparents is supporting the parents as they instruct their children so they will become successful adults who love God and follow Christ**. Beyond what's in these pages, we hope to explain many other points in subsequent books.*

For now, we encourage you to pray, pray some more, and then pray even more.

And, by all means, keep reading!

SECTION 3:
Three Practical Ways to Strengthen the Family Trinity

This section builds on the foundation of the Family Trinity to lay out practical principles for activities that grandparents should or should not do.

In particular, you'll learn about spoiling, baby-sitting, and gift-giving. In all three cases, our guidance differs from what the secular viewpoint says about these activities.

CHAPTER 8

No Spoiling Allowed

Proverbs 13:24 *He who spares the rod hates his son,*
but he who loves him is careful to discipline him.

Proverbs 23:13-14 *Do not withhold discipline from a child; if you*
punish him with the rod, he will not die. Punish him with the rod
and save his soul from death.

Like everyone else, we occasionally get an opportunity to listen to and advise some parents who are having difficulty with their children. In that setting, we learned from a young mother that she was having an issue concerning her toddler son and his grandmother who would occasionally look after him when regular day care wasn't available. It seemed that every time this happened, he would not cooperate with his parents when he got home and would eat next to nothing. Sometimes he even complained that his "tummy hurt."

When the mom finally asked the grandmother whether she had been giving treats to her son, the response revealed that she was inappropriately *giving him candy and chips because, "He said he was hungry." As the dialog ensued, she explained that she wanted her grandson to enjoy some freedom from the "rules" imposed on him at home.*

We were very pleased when we heard later that a heart-to-heart conversation between the two adults had cleared up this problem.

This chapter explains what happens when grandchildren are spoiled, and it isn't pretty. Despite this truth, American and other cultures seem to treat spoiling as a mandatory innocent behavior for grandparents toward their grandchildren. Because this attitude is so widespread, we suspect that all of us know of situations in which grandparents, maybe including ourselves, have spoiled the grandkids, at least for a little while.

Although we find that a lighthearted attitude toward spoiling is common, we also have determined that grandparents need to overcome it by realizing that spoiling works contrary to the important *godly* goal of building and maintaining long-term good, no, GREAT relationships with our grandchildren and their parents.

THERE'S NO RIGHT TO SPOIL

With no small amount of trepidation but plenty of confidence, we boldly contradict the conventional wisdom, especially (but not uniquely) in the United States, that the most important fundamental right of grandparents is spoiling their grandchildren!

Even while we were first-time expectant grandparents, we really didn't think this idea made any sense at all. Nonetheless, it seemed like everybody who learned about our situation (we confess, we may have told *some* of them what was coming) immediately said something like, "Oh, it's going to be so much fun to spoil your grandkids rotten." Another phrase that made us cringe is, "It'll be your job to sugar 'em up and send 'em home." Maybe our resistance reflected the fact that our grandparents didn't treat us that way and our parents didn't treat their grandkids like that. Whatever the reason might be, we've just never felt like spoiling can be a good idea.

After all, if our mission as grandparents is to *coach* our grandchildren's parents as they raise them up to be productive, successful God-loving and Christ-following adults, why would we want to throw a monkey wrench into the works by doing anything that cancels out what the parents are trying to help them learn?

WHAT IS "SPOILING"?

To begin, we offer up our definition of "spoiling":

> *Treating a person (young or old) in such a way that they develop a self-image of privilege, lack self-discipline, don't display accountability for their actions, and are in general obnoxious.*

We hope you can understand that the condition of being spoiled is not limited to children. Just think of some movie and music stars, athletes, business executives, and politicians, and you'll understand what we mean.

It's not a stretch to speculate that many of these adults are obnoxious, even horribly so, simply because that's the way they emerged from their childhood. On the other hand, who wouldn't be tempted to fall into that trap if they were to somehow become rich and famous? That's especially likely if they were always surrounded by fawning admirers or subordinates who continually reinforce their distorted sense of self-importance.

In any case, our point is that spoiling is *always* a bad idea.[3]

WHY DOES SPOILING HAPPEN?

We suggest that several common misconceptions lie behind the tendency of at least some, and perhaps many, grandparents to spoil their grandchildren.

- They're not confident the children will love them and want to be around them without bribes and other indulgences. In that case, the real problem is whatever originally shaped the grandparents' understanding of their role in the Family Trinity.

- They feel insecure simply because they fear that all children don't like older people.

- They may regret or even feel guilty over the way they treated their adult children when they were growing up by being too harsh or just not having enough money at the time to provide special things for their children. As a result, they believe they need to compensate by going overboard with their grandchildren.

In these situations, you can see that the grandparents' mistaken aim is to improve their own lives instead of supporting the parents' efforts to raise their children. As a result, it's not hard to recognize that *the young ones are being used instead of being loved!*

Surely, nothing can justify this behavior.

Apart from these explanations based on the grandparents' issues, it's also possible that they just think they need to spoil their grandchildren because that's what their grandparents did to them when they were young.

As a result, grandparents should assess their situation and then confront and resolve any spoiling issues quickly, if only for their own good. But, of course, it would not be just for their own good. Unless the Family Trinity is repaired to close this breach, it won't be able to have lasting positive effects for the parents, grandchildren, and many future generations to come.

If you find that you are a spoiling grandparent, don't be discouraged. Anyone can overcome these behaviors through deliberate efforts, including prayer and working with the parents and others. Now is the time to address the problem before it gets passed on to your grandchildren and then their grandchildren two generations later.

WHAT ABOUT "GOOD" SPOILING?

Certainly, there are appropriate times to give grandkids special treatment as an expression of genuine affection, love, and respect. Those actions can make great contributions to their self-confidence by showing them that someone in addition to their parents really, really loves them.

The key to success in this "good" spoiling is keeping the focus on the kids and giving them great experiences they'll remember during their lives and emulate when they become grandparents themselves.

So, how might you spoil your grandchildren the good way?

It's simple: just love them for who they are! Shower them with affection and give them lots and lots of time and attention. Talk to them… no, talk *with* them about what they're thinking and feeling. Find out what excites and interests them. Look for their special gifts and tendencies. Speak highly of their parents and, most of all, tell them how much God loves them and wants the best for them, too. Share with them lots of stories about your childhood and about their parents when they were kids.

By doing these things, grandparents will provide experiences that stimulate thoughts and emotions that in turn create lifelong memories;

ACTION POINT!

We also know you'll find great satisfaction and peace in occasionally bestowing a personal blessing on your grandchildren. Doing so affirms their value, girds their faith, and otherwise helps them face the future with confidence.

This blessing can be given at home in a simple setting where the grandparents set aside a special time to remind the children of their God-given gifts and strengths, of God's love for them, and His plans for their futures. The blessing should also commit the grandparents to be active in the grandchildren's lives through prayer and encouragement.

The high point of GrandCamp© is the time when grandparents bless their grandchildren in front of the other participating families. Experience shows that this public setting makes those commitments even more meaningful and bonding.[4]

after all, you're modeling for them how to be grandparents to your great-great-grandchildren.

AT A DISTANCE?

So, what should you do if you're a long distance away, or if some other reason keeps you from seeing your grandchildren very often?

Unfortunately, your first tendency might be to try to make up for the infrequency by indulging them to an extreme when you do get to see them. That's OK to some limited extent (like the first few minutes), but watch out. If it goes on any longer than that, perhaps you're just indulging yourself!

It's far wiser and better for everyone to make intentional efforts to communicate often with the parents and children. The distance between you won't seem so great if you use greeting cards, handwritten notes, phone calls (video calls are really good), emails, texting, social media, and whatever else is available to reach out to them.

When you do communicate this way, be sure your messages are full of encouragement for your grandchildren (and their parents) and questions about how they're doing. When they reach out to you, be sure your replies are both prompt and personal. Of course, you'll want to keep them informed about yourself, but please, please, don't dwell on your aches, pains, doctor visits, or complaints of other kinds! If you're really sick, you need to let them know, but spare them the minute details. As young people say, that's "TMI," or "Too Much Information."

Above all, don't pretend to be a young person with trendy text abbreviations and emojis. In all likelihood, you'll come across as an old person trying to act like something you aren't . . .

SUGAR COMES IN TWO KINDS

To capsulize this chapter, our encouragement to all grandparents is to always let kind words, gentle actions, and genuine affections be the "sugar" that we load up our grandchildren with before we "send them home."

Always, we must look out for the possibility that we are subconsciously satisfying our own needs. Instead, our job is to facilitate the incredibly important intergenerational process of supporting our adult children's efforts to prepare our grandchildren to be happy, faithful, and well-adjusted godly adults for the future.

---

3 For a brief but helpful explanation of spoiling, including symptoms, causes, and cures, see http://www.webmd.com/parenting/guide/spoiled-child#1. (Accessed in January 2017)

4 GrandCamp© is a program offered through Christian Grandparenting Network that offers retreats for a grandparent or grandparents to take their grandchildren (ages 7-12 are recommended) on a 5-day, 4-night adventure with other families at a comfortable facility. In addition to the spoken blessing, other activities include Bible stories, scripture memorization, games for everyone, separate kids' adventures while the adults attend short seminars on Christian grandparenting, and lots of fun. Every afternoon is set aside for each family to engage in their own special memory-building experiences. See www.grandcamps.org for more information. You can also contact the Network if your church or a group of churches would like to sponsor a camp in your area.

CHAPTER 9

You're More Than Free Baby-Sitters

Mark 10:7-9 *[Jesus taught]* " *'For this reason a man will leave his father and mother and be united to his wife, and the two will become one flesh.' So they are no longer two, but one . . ."*

By its very name, "baby-sitting" seems like an innocent and non-burdensome way for grandparents to help out. What harm can arise from doing that? Well, here are three short tales.

The first involves the arrival of an unplanned first baby to a couple who want to advance their careers by continuing to work fulltime. Because they think they can't afford to pay for professional daycare, they expect the grandparents to provide it every working day for free over at least the first 18 months.

The second involves parents who frequently decide to have supposedly "spontaneous" date nights and always call the grandparents at the last minute to come sit with the kids so they can go out.

The third involves a grandmother with four grandchildren in one family. In a regular cycle, each of them in turn stays overnight in her home every Friday. She's overjoyed that she has this regular one-on-one interaction with them.

Although these three scenarios seem like examples of grandparents' kindness, we'll show that each of them may not be as beneficial as it might seem.

Our primary aim in this chapter is to help grandparents realize that their role in the Family Trinity does not include constantly being imposed upon (and physically drained) by serving as *on-call baby sitters* for their grandchildren.

THREE REASONS

We have three reasons for bringing this advice to your attention.

First, the parents of our grandchildren need to learn to be more resourceful so they can solve their problems without relying on us. We know that their lives can be complex at times, but it's also just way too easy for them to always call Mom and Dad to the rescue.

To express this thought another way, it isn't good for our adult children to view us as their always available yet unpaid nannies or chauffeurs. For one thing, it does not promote a higher respect for us. For another, the quoted scripture at the beginning of this chapter tells us, and our adult children, that they need to grow up and away from us so that they can become successful adults on their own. If they're always turning to us for baby-sitting and picking up the kids, they're actually hindering their own normal development. By still depending on us, they're not enhancing their abilities to manage their family's activities without us.

Second, if parents rely too much on grandparents as baby-sitters, they can be making it harder for their children (our grandchildren) to learn how to behave and interact appropriately with older people who are not family members. Because they are or will be under the instruction and custody of teachers, athletic coaches, doctors, and even police officers, for example, they need to learn how to respond to direction and discipline from other authority figures. One way for that lesson to be learned is by using baby sitters other than us.

Third, we sincerely hope you grandparents have plenty of other things going on in your daily life that involve stimulation, recreation, ministries, and service to others who are not part of your family. All of us should still want to lead our own lives with our own interests outside the family. However, if we're tied down all the time as baby-sitters, we may be missing out on other important experiences and ways to help other people.

If you haven't already anticipated it, yet another reason for not baby-sitting all the time is that we're all getting older and probably finding it harder to put forth the effort it takes to chase after kids while we entertain, supervise, and feed them, not to mention change their diapers.

Notice that we use the phrase "*on-call* baby sitters." For sure, having alone time with the grandchildren is certainly one of the joys of grandparenthood. Our advice is that, to the extent possible, you'll want to

ACTION POINT!

We know of grandparents, including us, who seek out situations (such as, but not limited to GrandCamp® retreats) in which only one or two of their grandchildren are under their care while the others (if any) are at home or involved in another activity that is more age-appropriate. There's nothing wrong with that, for sure!

We like these situations because they provide special one-on-one or two-on-two encounters that produce great moments and memories. Therefore, we encourage you to either initiate them or respond positively when asked. Just manage how often they occur to be sure they remain exceptional. You also don't want to make it harder for their entire family unit to have their own times together.

ensure that these occasions are always special by not letting them happen so frequently that they become routine.

SPECIAL SITUATIONS

On the other hand, all grandparents need to acknowledge that some unfortunate situations can justify different practices from those we just described. Specifically, such things as military deployments and financial, health, or relationship difficulties may compel grandparents to become regular day-care providers. Unusual sacrifices may be appropriate under these circumstances.

Once things settle down, different and more permanent arrangements should be established to ensure that the grandparents' own health and well-being are not placed at risk.

Whenever these sorts of situations arise, it's essential that expectations be clearly established for everyone, both parents and grandparents, so that they all clearly understand and respect any limitations on the grandparents' availability. It doesn't do anyone any good if these alternate care-givers are so worn out that they need their own assistance!

TOO MUCH OF A GOOD THING?

Perhaps it will surprise some when we suggest that it's possible to do so much baby-sitting that it's bad for the grandchildren and their parents. For one thing, being *too* available may somehow enable the parents to dysfunctionally devote themselves to their careers and other activities instead of their families. We still wince about another situation in which friends asked for our advice about whether they should keep their single-mom daughter's children so she could have what she called a "party weekend" getaway.

We know some grandparents will say there's no problem if they're frequently called on to help out because they just love looking after the grandchildren. Who doesn't?

What we're warning against is the possibility that parents' calls to baby-sit can be overdone. If you think that's happening (you'll sense it before the parents do), have an adult-to-adult conversation with them to be sure you're supporting them in fulfilling their family obligations and that you aren't being exploited in a way that allows them to avoid those responsibilities.

Our consistent reminder is that the chief grandparenting responsibility is helping the parents raise good and productive citizens who love Jesus. None of us has the duty of making our life more stressful to make theirs less so!

WATCH OUT!

Strange as it may seem, grandparents can make themselves too available or invite themselves into the baby-sitting role too often. These situations can arise if the grandparents indulge their own desires to be with the grandkids so much that they diminish the amount of family time they have with their mom, dad and siblings.

As mentioned in one of the opening stories for this chapter, we met a grandmother who was so excited about her tradition of having each of her four grandchildren spend a night with her every Friday and the next day. In retrospect, we wish we had asked her (with a big smile) whether the children's family ever enjoys a weekend that includes all four of them at the same time.

Knowing who she is, we think this was a case where she just wasn't aware of her action's consequences. Any of us could fall into this trap, so once more, we strongly urge you not to let something as innocent as baby-sitting get out of hand before you realize it too late.

CHAPTER 10

The In's and Out's of Gracious Gift-Giving

Proverbs 13:22 *A good man leaves an inheritance for his children's children...*

1 Timothy 6:17-18 *Command those who are rich in this present world not to be arrogant nor to put their hope in wealth . . . Command them to do good, to be rich in good deeds, and to be generous and willing to share.*

We heard of a situation in which a couple was completely blown away when one of their widowed mothers arrived at Christmas with three very large gift-wrapped boxes. It turned out she had brought each grandchild their very own television set to have in their rooms. Besides creating a very awkward situation because the kids loved the gifts but the parents didn't want the TVs in their house, the grandmother's heart-breaking explanation was that she thought these expensive gifts would help the children love her.

One form of spoiling is thoughtlessly giving lavish gifts. We know this observation is touchy because it may raise some hackles. Perhaps we're going against the flow of modern culture, at least in America, but we're going to do it anyway!

WHAT COULD BE WRONG IN GIVING GIFTS?

It's no surprise that grandparents' giving of gifts to their grandchildren is generally viewed as their *privilege*. We don't dispute this point, but we do believe that gift-giving must be done responsibly to avoid doing harm.

As we see it, grandparents can give either *lavishly* or *graciously*. The difference between the two styles doesn't have to do with how many gifts or how expensive they are. Rather, the distinction lies in the motives of the givers!

Lavish giving occurs when the givers are seeking their own ends by giving out of guilt, insecurity, pride, and/or a need for attention. In contrast, *gracious* giving occurs when the givers are serving others by providing for needs, wants, and special memories, all out of a spirit of sincere love for the recipients.

In other words, and contrary to a materialistic culture's beliefs, lavish gifts are actually poor gifts that reflect self-centered motives, not a generous heart. Like God's love, gracious giving is intended to build up others and call attention to Him, the giver of all good gifts!

Thus, the answer to the question of "What could be wrong in giving gifts?" is that they can be given for the wrong reasons.

OTHER GIVING PROBLEMS

Like the grandmother in the opening story, some grandparents act as if they have the *inalienable right* to give lavishly to their grandchildren without being held accountable for the gifts they give or why they gave them. We're also saddened by situations in which some grandparents feel *obligated* to give lavishly, even if they can ill afford it.

Unfortunately, some grandparents may use lavish giving to their grandchildren to somehow soothe their own nagging guilt from not being able to give material items to their adult children when they were young. Others may do it because they think the grandchildren will love them in proportion to the number and kinds of gifts they receive.

In still other circumstances, especially with broken or blended families, misguided grandparents may use their gifts in *competition* with the parents and the other grandparents to prove they're more loving, generous, and wealthy than everyone else. Sadly, this motive can produce just the opposite result because it's usually transparent to all, even the kids, if not right away then eventually.

Also, grandparents who are separated by geographical distance may feel like they need to make up for their absence by spending lots of money. That idea simply makes no sense because there are lots of ways to be in touch with them.

It's also time for a conversation with the grandchildren's parents if they have come to expect the grandparents to go overboard instead of providing gifts from their own budgets.

In all these cases, little or no sincerity accompanies the gifts. As such, the grandparents are being neither good coaches to the parents nor good models for the grandchildren.

Beyond a doubt, the worst outcome of lavish gift-giving occurs when the grandchildren come to *identify* their grandparents as nothing more than immense cornucopias whose main role in their young lives is ensuring that all their wants and needs are met. Because the grandchildren look to the grandparents as models of how they should be when their children have children, then they may find themselves compelled to give lavishly without even understanding why.

GIVING WITH GRACE

Instead of self-centered lavish giving, we encourage grandparents to engage in others-centered *gracious* giving that conveys to the grandchildren that their gifts come from the givers' hearts as expressions of their love and concern for their well-being.

To accomplish gracious giving, then, those who give the gifts must give them out of pure motives, not with any ulterior or other self-serving purpose. Their generosity must not be for show or pretense but genuine with no inappropriate purposes. As Paul wrote to Timothy in the passage for this chapter: "Command those who are rich in this present world not to be arrogant nor to put their hope in wealth . . . Command them to do good, to be rich in good deeds, and to be generous and willing to share."

We're certain that giving with grace clearly demonstrates to those who receive the gifts that they are fully and completely loved. When they comprehend how much they're loved, they're released to accept a material item as a token of the giver's true feelings. When that happens, they will cherish it instead of considering it to be a tawdry possession to be used for only a little while and then tossed aside and forgotten.

To achieve this result, we believe grandparents should approach gift-giving carefully and prayerfully. They should examine their motives, not just their bank balance and their budget. They should take time and effort to come to a full understanding of what their grandchildren truly need and want, not what they say they "just have to have!"

GIVING WITH HARMONY
To be gracious givers to our grandchildren, we grandparents should seek close harmony with both them *and* their parents. We need to establish beyond doubt in all their minds and hearts that we love them unconditionally. When that truth is settled, then our gifts can reflect our joy from knowing they feel the same way toward us. Beyond that concept, there are very practical reasons to be in sync with the parents.

Suppose, for example, that a grandchild had expressed a desire to the parents for a particular item, such as a special building block set or another plaything. Suppose further that Mom and Dad decided to harness the power of this desire to create a meaningful learning situation by agreeing they would give the child small cash rewards for performing additional chores and tasks with a positive attitude. These cash rewards over a month or two would be enough to buy the item. Wow! What a great opportunity to instill responsibility, create pride in accomplishment, and give the child the valuable experience of satisfying a deferred desire. That's the sort of arrangement that grandparents should support and nurture!

But think how this opportunity would be ruined if the grandparents stepped in, either deliberately or unwittingly, and bought the desired toy and just gave it to the grandchild. It would be even worse if they went overboard and bought an item that's more extravagant than the one the child wanted.

Consider the potential consequences.

- First, the parents' teaching points would be completely lost.

- Second, that lost positive lesson would be replaced by a negative lesson that communicates to the child, "You only need to wait for somebody to give you whatever you want without working for it."

- Third, it makes the parents look weak and unloving in their children's eyes because they couldn't, or wouldn't, meet their desires.

- Fourth, the grandchildren will view their grandparents as one of those overflowing and inexhaustible cornucopias.

Without harmony between the parents and the grandparents, gift-giving can be terribly abused if the givers try to outdo everyone else to show they can give the most. The likely outcome of engaging in this kind of behavior is warped children who grow up to be warped adults.

GIVING FROM A DISTANCE
If you live far from your grandchildren, do your best to give them your *presence* instead of *presents*! If possible, travel to be with them on their birthday or Christmas or other gift-giving occasion. This action and

sacrifice will model for them how much you love them far more clearly than any material thing ever could. As a bonus, the memories will last a whole lot longer, maybe even for generations.

ACTION 🌰 POINT!

Because the grandparents' goal should be supporting the parents' efforts to raise well-adjusted and productive adults, good gift-giving is rooted in great communication with the parents.

It begins by letting them know that we're on their side in their important task of instructing their children and that we don't want our gift-giving behavior to be contrary to the values they're trying to develop.

Thus, we offer up this important principle: *always, always, always, ask the parents what they want their children to have instead of asking your grandchildren what they want.*

It is also very important to figure out or have candid discussions about how much the parents themselves will be spending so the kids will see their gifts as the most generous.

Above all, work hard to discover and endorse, if appropriate, the positive lessons their parents are trying to teach your grandchildren about eternal and otherwise intangible things as compared to material things. Then diligently cooperate with them so you don't ruin their plans. If you think the parents are overemphasizing material stuff, don't fall into the trap of trying to please *them* by giving your grandchildren extravagant gifts.

Naturally, these conversations can create wonderful opportunities to provide some good coaching for the parents.

Of course, if it isn't feasible or possible for you to travel, then do all you can to be in close communication. If you're up to it, use technology to see and be seen in their home as well as to hear and be heard.

As we've described, the real work behind giving is planning it carefully and thoughtfully. Your love can come shining through even if you're not there to hand over your gifts. Above all, don't slip into lavish giving to make up for your absence!

If you do want to give generously with good motives, we suggest you provide simpler tangible gifts to the grandchildren and go overboard with contributions to, say, their *college funds*. Even though the kids won't understand what you've done until they start to realize that education after high school is important and expensive, just think how pleased and excited they will be when they learn that you've been helping them out all along. Never mind that you might not be around to receive their thanks; after all, you're supposed to boost their well-being, not your ego.

JUST FOR CLARITY

We want to be sure no one is confused about what we mean by "lavish" giving. After all, the Apostle John praises God when he begins the third chapter of his first epistle by crying out, "How great is the love the Father has lavished on us, that we should be called children of God!"

The Greek word that he used for "lavished" carries the sense that God gives us His love out of an abundance, not with the attitude that He is trying to win our love in return.

Scripture is just full of proof that God gives us everything through His grace (*charis*) as an expression of His *agape* love. And so it should be with us.

Thus, we declare that we cannot overemphasize the blessings that will come to grandparents who sincerely give only as an expression of their love without selfishness, insecurity, guilt or other wrong motive. The reason for presenting the gifts completely overpowers the number and cost of the gifts.

DIGGING INTO THE WORD!

Luke 21:1-4 presents Jesus's teaching on the principle that the reason for giving, whether sound or unsound, is what matters to Him:

> As he looked up, Jesus saw the rich putting their gifts into the temple treasury. He also saw a poor widow put in two very small copper coins. "I tell you the truth," he said, "this poor widow has put in more than all the others. All these people gave their gifts out of their wealth; but she out of her poverty put in all she had to live on."

The convicting point is that the widow was declaring to God how much she loved Him while the others were giving lavishly so that everyone could see how wealthy and important they were. Jesus didn't care a whit for their gifts. As a result of his praise, to this day, people are still reading about the widow's sincere heart and marveling at her humility.

The old saying is right: It truly is "the thought that counts!"

SUMMING IT UP

Gracious gift-giving expresses and builds healthy and long-lasting love throughout the whole Family Trinity. More importantly, it reflects the gracious gifts we receive from God every day of our lives.

In stark contrast, lavish and other poorly motivated gift-giving corrupts both the givers and the recipients. It can never build love and can easily lead to unhealthy expectations and dependencies. If you want to be "great grandparents," just don't go down that path!

SECTION 4:
Special Situations

This section only touches on a few of the challenging circumstances that some, even many, families may find themselves having to deal with.

The specific topics include (1) family structures with special architectures, including adoptive, fostering, and multicultural situations, as well as (2) dealing with tragic situations involving missing, disinterested, and struggling parents.

We make no pretense that we have fully described the pain and heartache that accompany these situations or that we have all the answers to the problems these families encounter. Our goal is simply to alert all of us to the possibilities we face in a broken world and to encourage those who find themselves having to deal with those challenges.

CHAPTER 11

On Being Adoptive, Foster and/or Cross-Cultural Grandparents

Psalm 82:3-4 *Defend the cause of the weak and fatherless; maintain the rights of the poor and oppressed. Rescue the weak and needy; deliver them from the hand of the wicked.*

James 1:27 *Religion that God our Father accepts as pure and faultless is this: to look after orphans and widows in their distress ...*

Around 1990, we (Diana and Paul) began to feel pangs that it was too early for us to be looking at an "empty nest." With good counsel, we looked into international adoption but then backed away for reasons that were never very clear to us. Then, three years later, with one son soon headed to college and the other two years away from doing the same, we prayed again and discovered that hundreds of thousands of children were in orphanages in Russia and that the government had become more open to adoption. We were intrigued and then clearly called to go ahead. Before long, we were matched with an active three year-old named Angela, who charmed us in her video with foot-long eyelashes, snapping brown eyes, and a smile that melted everything in sight.

Through a series of stop-and-go miraculous events that deserve their own book, we had to go to Russia twice but brought her home shortly after her fourth birthday. Thus began an amazing journey in our family as all five of us tackled the task of growing by adoption, not by biological birth. We cannot begin to describe all that happened, but we will say two things. First, adoption in real life is not as it appears in movies and Anne of Green Gables, and second, all the hard work is well worth it to save a life and bring someone not only into our family but also into the family of God. The rest of the story is yet to be told as Angie is (at the time we're writing) in her mid-20's, working in criminal justice and newly married.

We think you'll find our own story has given us a good platform for writing this chapter on the various, and always special, ways that God uses to build some Family Trinities.

OUT OF THE SHADOWS

When the two of us were young children, the word "adoption" was whispered rather than openly discussed. In those days, an adopted child was pitied and not easily accepted, not only in society but even in the family. There were still institutions called "orphanages" and "children's homes" to which unfortunate youngsters were transferred – often akin to being incarcerated and otherwise kept out of public view. Further, it was rare to encounter marriages between men and women from different racial and national heritages. As we all know, in 21st century America, and in many other cultures, these attitudes have been replaced by more accepting and appreciative ones.

We also remind you that Asaph the Psalmist was making this point thousands of years ago, as evidenced by the verses from Psalm 82 that we quote at the beginning of the chapter: "Defend the cause of the *weak and fatherless*; maintain the rights of the *poor and oppressed*. Rescue the *weak and needy*; deliver them from the hand of the wicked." These words make it clear that God commands us to care for those who are without adequate resources and otherwise vulnerable.

In addition to our story in the opening, we can write on this subject with some authority because our current three-generation extended family of sixteen includes our internationally adopted daughter, two multiracial marriages (including one that is international), and four dual citizens. We know we're not alone, and we expect the future will see more families with an eclectic population like ours.

ADOPTIVE GRANDPARENTING

We'll begin our explanation of adoption at the place where we started on our own journey: it is clearly part of God's plan for the lives of many.

To begin, consider how the Apostle Paul explained to Christians in Ephesians 1:5 that God "predestined us to be *adopted* as his sons [and daughters] through Jesus Christ, in accordance with his pleasure and will." If God has adopted us to redeem us out of a hopeless state, then surely He would want us to do the same to rescue children who are desperately alone!

Here also is the declaration in James 1 that we quoted above: "Religion that God our Father accepts as pure and faultless is this: to look after *orphans* and widows in their distress . . ."

We know that being adoptive parents isn't for everyone, and families who contemplate adopting need to give this decision intense prayer-filled consideration with advice from wise friends and family, trusted counselors, and, where possible, others who have been through this experience. Of course, if you have pursued your role as a grandparent who coaches your adult children, both your advice and blessing will be especially helpful if they are thinking about adopting.

ACTION POINT!

Perhaps nothing drives adoptive parents to distraction as much as the common *faux pas* of referring to their biological children as their "own" children to distinguish them from their adopted children. In the eyes of the law, but more importantly in the eyes of God and the parents, the adopted child is also the parents' own child.

All this discussion leads us to suggest that you may very well end up as *adoptive grandparents*. If that should be true for you, may we offer two pieces of practical advice?

First, it's vital that you accept an adopted grandchild as an essential component of God's amazing architecture for your family. Certainly, he or she has been added to your family for their own benefit. In addition, you must always realize that God is also changing and improving the parents, the siblings, and even the grandparents. Therefore, we urge you to accept, love, cherish, and embrace these children as part of your family.

Second, you can anticipate that your adopted grandkids will be different in several ways. They may have a distinctive outward appearance, an accent (if they are adopted sometime after infancy), unfamiliar thought processes, and unusual behavior patterns. Don't let these differences fool you; even if you believe your DNA is pretty good, you'll be surprised that this grandchild who doesn't have any of it is probably better at some things than any of your biological grandchildren!

ACTION POINT!

If your adult children come to you for counsel on adopting (and they probably will if you have a good relationship with them), remember to listen before speaking and then only ask questions that will cause them to articulate their thoughts as they explain what they're thinking about doing.

In other words, don't start offering advice until they ask for it, and, above all, *don't* recommend against moving ahead. Instead, assure them of your support one way or another. If necessary, it's OK, indeed, essential, to warn them that real-life adoption is not like it's portrayed on television and in the movies. It's hard and often tough and heart-breaking work, but it is God's work, and none of us should be afraid of it.

Of course, none of those differences matter when it comes to their need for love and their right to be loved, so you have to do your part and love them, period.

Always remember that the main role for grandparents is to support the parents. In the case of adoptive parents, that role expands because of the potential for new doubts and frustrations for them as the child comes into the family and, in all certainty, disrupts its previous patterns and customs. In these situations, grandparents are called on to be patient and ready to offer their wisdom on how to cope with those problems. Without going out on a limb, we know the parents certainly need more emotional support under these circumstances.

Here's our bottom line on being an adoptive grandparent: it's not significantly different from being a biological grandparent because (a) God put this child in your family and (b) you will love him or her with all your heart. If (b) isn't true, then we're afraid something might be holding you back that shouldn't be. . .

DIGGING INTO THE WORD!

We invite you to carefully consider Paul's words in Ephesians 2:8-10, especially the final phrase: "For it is by grace you have been saved, through faith – and this not from yourselves, it is the gift of God – not by works, so that no one can boast. For we are God's workmanship, created in Christ Jesus to do good works, which *God prepared in advance for us to do.*"

If adoption is one of those good works that God has prepared for your adult children (and you, as their coach), then they should go for it and you should be kneeling beside them and standing behind them!

FOSTER GRANDPARENTING

The role of *foster grandparent* is increasingly common. With so many children in unsafe, vulnerable, or other at-risk situations, your adult offspring may choose to step into this important and challenging emergency custody role.

Because foster arrangements are often temporary, you might think there isn't much of a role for you as a grandparent. To the contrary, the stress and confusion felt by foster children make it necessary for them to be surrounded by as many loving and caring adults as they can handle. At the very least, you may find occasions to take over some of the parents' regular responsibilities (shopping, cooking, cleaning, and caring for any other grandchildren) so they can focus on the children's immediate needs with fewer distractions. Even in that limited role, you will have plenty of opportunities to establish a relationship with the children that will help them understand they are safe and protected in their new location.

In some cases, foster children may be placed with a family for a longer term because the risk that forced them into foster care cannot be easily resolved. If this happens in your family, you may find yourself in a much deeper relationship with a stronger attachment to the children. This response is normal because you will see and interact with them more times and in a variety of circumstances. Heed all the advice and guidelines provided by the social service agency that places the children in the home to ensure that you're always doing what is best for them.

In many cases, circumstances can make it suitable for foster children to eventually be adopted into their foster families. If that happens in your case, you will be transformed into an adoptive grandparent, and you will be even more inclined to take a deep interest in the children and do more for them and their parents.

Please note, however, that the bonding process and other adjustments are not necessarily going to go more smoothly simply because the children have lived with the adoptive family before being adopted. The

ACTION POINT!

As with adoption, success with foster children is never going to be as simple and beautiful as it's portrayed in fictional stories. In many cases, the children may be pulled from the foster home and returned to the birth family in what remains an inferior situation, as awful as that might seem.

Because of this possibility, some might think it would be a good idea to hold back early in the process so that you won't make a loving commitment to the children. However, doing that would be just the opposite of what you need to do. It might just be your love and the love of your adult children that pulls the foster children through a heart-breaking and gut-wrenching experience.

Fortunately, you can also be there in this situation to support your family as they grieve the loss of these beloved children. They will need you to help them cope with the frustration that comes from working with a system that seems to view at-risk young people more like property than vulnerable human beings who have the right to be loved and cared for.

bonding process for the children is much more complicated than it is for the parents. For one thing, the parents have a deeper understanding of what is going on, while the children have probably been living in fear and without trustworthy adults around, and perhaps even with abusive adults. They will have many heavy psychological and emotional questions that will take years to be suitably answered. In fact, some of them might never be answered. You will love them anyway, so don't worry about that part!

CROSS-CULTURAL GRANDPARENTING
Obviously, foreign adoptions like ours create *cross-cultural grandparents* as well. You may also enter into this status if your adult child marries a

person from another culture, which can mean they came from another country or a different culture from within your own country. Our daughter made our family cross-cultural when she arrived from Russia when she was four. Our son did the same thing when he married a wonderful woman from the Philippines and they made us cross-cultural grandparents when their first son was born.

Don't be confused on this point that applies to children adopted from another country, even as tiny babies: they almost always have an innate interest and pride in their origins. Even if they become naturalized citizens and have no memory of living elsewhere, they really care about where they came from. We find the same is true for children born to a parent from another country, like our two grandsons.

Knowing that this longing exists, don't be surprised when their parents go to great lengths to include some of the original country's customs, foods, and language in the family's daily lives. You need to welcome these practices, too. It's among the best things you can do for the parents and all the grandchildren.

SUMMING UP

Here's our concluding advice: look on any adopted, foster, and/or cross-cultural grandchildren through God's eyes and you'll see that He doesn't show preferences for any specific biological origins, skin color,

---

ACTION 🌰 POINT!

Don't be aloof when other cultures enter into your family. Be adventurous and embracing. You may believe your country, whichever one it might be, is the greatest of them all. But that opinion doesn't mean that only its ways are good and great. And it also doesn't mean that an adopted child will automatically express gratitude at being taken out of their birth country. As with all adoptions, the child's feelings are more complex than most people believe.

language, or nationality. He made each of us in His image and He loves all of us more than we can comprehend.

Therefore, it should not be a huge leap into unfamiliar territory for us to love all our grandchildren as He loves them, regardless of where they come from or the process by which they came into our family.

CHAPTER 12

Standing in the Gap: It's Tough

Ephesians 4:1 … *I urge you to live a life worthy of the calling you have received.*

Ephesians 2:10 *For we are God's workmanship, created in Christ Jesus to do good works, which God prepared in advance for us to do.*

Philippians 4:13 *I can do everything through him [Christ] who gives me strength.*

Simone Biles, winner of four gold medals and a single bronze in gymnastics, was unquestionably among the American heroines in the 2016 Olympic Games.

"Black, poor, fatherless, with a drug-addicted mother," syndicated columnist Star Parker wrote, "Biles was saved by Christian love. Her mother's father and his wife pulled her from the bosom of disaster. They adopted her and her sister, took them to their home, became their mom and *dad, gave Simone Christian home schooling and transmitted the values that built this incredible young woman."*

Because of her grandparents' love and commitment to pour their lives into her, Simone rose with confidence to achieve what few people have achieved. Her grandparents saved her life and showed her Christ's love in very tangible ways.

Of course, not all children raised by their grandparents will become Olympic gold medalists! Yet, the unselfish love of godly grandparents combined with consistent actions can make a huge difference in what the grandchildren will become. Imagine what Simone's life could have been like if her grandparents had not stepped up to "stand in the gap" in the Family Trinity that was created when her parents were unable to meet their responsibilities.

NO ONE ASKS FOR THIS

At this point in the book, it's time to confront the very difficult situations that can compel grandparents to assume many of the responsibilities for the grandchildren that should belong to the parents.

Tragically, the reality is that more families than ever are falling into this category. Here are three of the biggest challenges that grandparents in such situations may face:

- Something dreadful has taken one or both parents out of the picture.

- The parents are not fully engaged and not fulfilling their responsibilities.

- The grandchildren are not learning about Jesus from their parents.

We'll take them one at a time. Of course, we can't possibly cover each situation in this book to the level of detail they deserve. We also know that each family's situation and circumstances are different. As a result, all we can do is draw some generalities and offer a great deal of sympathy for the burdens carried by grandparents who answer the call to stand in the gap when the Family Trinity is incomplete.

PARENTS OUT OF THE PICTURE

When I (Paul) was eight years old, my mother died from cancer she contracted long before I was born as her fourth and final child. Unfortunately, people in those days didn't tell their children much about death and disease, so her departure was sudden, unexpected, and terribly traumatic for me and my three older siblings. I still remember waking up one morning to the sound of my brothers' and sister's crying and then my father whispering the terrible news to me. It was beyond my comprehension, but we were comforted by the presence of my father's parents and his brother and his wife. Soon, neighbors and church friends were in the house. I even recall the shock of seeing my third grade teacher in my living room with tears in her eyes.

After a few days, a funeral, and lots of hugs and head pats, it was back to school and picking up the pieces. I was also wonderfully consoled by our African-American housekeeper, Viola Garner, who I so look forward to seeing again in heaven so I can give her proper thanks and tell her what she now means to me.

The pain began to ease a couple years later when my father remarried a very brave 30-year old woman who came into a family with four kids ranging now from 17 to 10. What a welcome addition she was!

Beyond a doubt, the most helpful people in those first two years were my dad's parents, who lived only about 15 minutes away in Houston, and my mother's mother, who lived in Des Moines, a very long train ride away. That inconvenience did not stop her from coming several times in the first two years, and she still came many times later and was warmly welcomed by my stepmother.

As tragic as it was, this sort of thing happens all the time for lots of different reasons, leaving children without one or even both their parents. Whether the specific cause is death, disability, divorce, or something else, such as a military deployment or even incarceration, grandparents can, and should, step up to a higher level of involvement. They'll be needed for some of the things that parents normally do, of course. What's more important is to make their own loving contributions to their grandchildren's adjustment to the tragedy. Clearly, some grandchildren will benefit from professional counseling, as well.

In my case, my grandparents stepped into our family's gap and filled it with love. Their presence, affection, and stability helped all of us get through a really rough time.

In cases where one parent is left, we're certain the grandparents should step up to provide the essential love and support without regard to whether that person is related by birth or by marriage. Either way, he or she will feel devastated and alone, just like the children. The grandparents can help every family member know they are loved and that their grief, confusion, frustration, and anger are normal, shared, and surmountable.

The support may take on different forms. Here are four:

- *Emotional:* Being steady, yet sympathetic, allows grandparents to assist their grandchildren in regaining their sense of stability.

- *Time and effort:* Helping with chores, and just being there and otherwise available, frees the grieving family to focus on the really important things.

- *Financial:* If there is a need for money to get through the adjustment phase, grandparents should be ready to help out as they are able without expecting to be repaid.

- *Spiritual:* Through gentle and sincere words about God's ability to comfort and bring peace, grandparents can help soothe hurting hearts. Bible verses and wisdom can bring peace and assurance. However, they also should be prepared to deal with the challenging question of, "Why did God let this happen to us?"

Certainly, the grandparents' prayers can help them and all the others. Praying together with the grandchildren and the rest of the family will be a powerful witness to them as well.

In contrast to a loss through death, divorce can be very awkward and difficult to deal with. In what is now a divided family, helpful grandparents always remember that their first obligation is to help their grandchildren become successful God-loving adults. When divorce occurs, fulfilling that responsibility means, to the extent possible, maintaining good relationships with each parent and continuing to help them both as they look after their children. This continuity is essential because, in all likelihood, the grandchildren will feel confused, unconfident, overwhelmed, and even guilty. They clearly need the additional stability and consistency that perhaps only grandparents can provide. Our job in that role is to be available to them, even as we suffer in our own confusion and grief. In the midst of heartache, remember Philippians 4:13 – "I can do *everything* through him [Christ] who gives me strength."

As bad as death and divorce are, the worst occurs when both parents are removed or incapacitated. In such cases, grandparents may have to assume full responsibility for their grandchildren's care and nurturing. We are personally familiar with several situations in which this elevation of responsibility has happened to close friends, and we stand amazed at and salute their courageous, tough choices to drastically adjust their own lives for the sake of the grandchildren.

This decision must not be made impulsively or out of guilt because the commitment can be very long-term and very demanding in a variety of ways. We recommend that there be much counsel, introspection, and intense prayer before taking on this role. Without steadfastness on the part of the grandparents, resentment can creep into their hearts, especially when emotional and physical fatigue build up. Everyone who stands in this gap must have deep wells of external support, including friends, peers in similar situations, other family members, church members, and professional counselors. Without such resources, it will be really difficult to live up to all those responsibilities. Of course, prayer by the grandparents and others can work wonders in these circumstances.

ACTION POINT!

There isn't much that one can actually do before the unexpected happens, but it does make sense to occasionally stop and talk among yourselves about what you might be called on to do. If there is time, be sure to discuss with the parents what they would like to have done. However, like it says in the TV commercial, "Life comes at you fast," and none of us can ever be fully ready to stand in this sort of gap.

Also, we find that it's important to ensure the children have their own circles of support they can draw on, especially later. Some day when the younger children get to the age of increased awareness, they'll notice that the adults who are looking after them at home are a great deal older than their friends' parents. As a result, they should have other adults in their lives who are younger than their grandparents, such as athletic coaches, teachers, youth activity leaders, and other mentors. These friends will also be especially helpful if and when the grandparents can no longer carry the burdens or are themselves no longer living.

DISENGAGED PARENTS

In many respects, dealing with parents who are disengaged from their families can be much more difficult for grandparents than dealing with absent parents, primarily because the parents can negatively influence both the children and the grandparents' efforts to help them develop into good adults.

As a result, grandparents in this situation must draw on reservoirs of patience and diplomacy that they may not even know they have. As much as grandparents might want to take their adult children and their spouses by the shoulders and shake some sense into them, or just admonish them, it's improbable that doing so would ever accomplish anything worthwhile. In fact, actions like those are more likely to produce complete rejection and the loss of any influence the grandparents might have on the grandchildren.

Unfortunately, the details aren't any easier to describe, and we (Paul and Diana) are lacking much in the way of specific advice. Among other reasons for that frustration is the fact that each case is not just complicated but also completely different from all others. For example, the reason for the disengagement can impact how much grandparents are allowed into the parents' and grandchildren's lives. As a case in point, if the grandparents are perceived as a cause of what's not working in the family, then they're probably going to be completely cut off. Even if they are allowed some access into the children's lives, they might not be allowed to enter certain areas.

Above all, then, grandparents must do their best to avoid being shut out of the grandchildren's lives, even if that means not just biting their lips but gnawing them, and then swallowing so much pride that they get stomachaches. The grandchildren's interests and needs must always come first, and grandparents can help only when they have access that allows them to bring some of the stability and guidance the children aren't getting from their parents.

Being allowed into the family circle may mean having to agree that certain topics are off-limits. As distasteful as that arrangement might seem, the grandparents will have to abide by those boundaries in order to have an opportunity to help the grandchildren in other ways.

Our bottom line is that most, if not all, grandparents will not know exactly what to do when they're put into these circumstances. However, if they go about what they're doing in a prayerful and God-driven gentle spirit of love without being judgmental, they may be able to help the grandchildren cope with the situation and emerge from their childhood able to function at a high level.

Certainly, most grandparents will want to eventually try to help the disengaged parents change. However, if that transformation ever occurs, it will surely take much time and effort under difficult and tenuous conditions. In fact, and sadly, it is often beyond the grandparents' ability to accomplish.

ACTION POINT!

As best as they can, grandparents need to gently confront disengaged parents to learn where they're allowed to go in their conversations with them and the grandchildren. If this common ground is not identified, what the grandparents consider to be legitimate topics may prove to be hot buttons that should be avoided at all costs. On the other hand, the parents may surprise the grandparents with what they will allow. Without clarity ahead of time as to which is which, a false step could lead to all sorts of trouble.

Did we mention prayer?

Even though we've already mentioned it, we'll emphasize that prayer is essential and effective for all concerned.

BRINGING JESUS TO THE GRANDCHILDREN

Ideally, and even in the non-ideal sinful world in which we live, grandparents can be helpful reinforcements for their grandchildren's parents as they attempt to raise their kids in what Ephesians 6:4 describes as "the nurture and admonition of the Lord."

If the parents are Christ-followers, then grandparents should be ready to support them as they introduce their children to Jesus. At the risk of sounding spongy, it does no good to stew about denominations or other affiliations as long as the fundamental doctrines are there. After all, the group of believers the parents associate with might have some things more together than the grandparents' church!

What's the best way for the grandparents to help in this circumstance? Simply by loving their grandchildren and treating them in a way that expresses Jesus's love, hands, feet, heart, and voice to them. Frequent enthusiastic encouragement to their parents is also key.

In contrast to this happy situation, what do believing grandparents need to do when they have to stand in the gap that's created when their grandchildren are not being introduced to Jesus by their parents?

Our first observation is that there are no easy or formulaic answers. Because every case is unique, our general advice to grandparents in this situation is to be very sensitive to the Holy Spirit's leading for their spoken words (or silence) and active deeds (or non-deeds).

Above all, we urge grandparents in this situation to take deep comfort in the fact that no one has ever been saved by their grandparents. Only the Holy Spirit can accomplish salvation for the grandchildren, and He can perform that miracle in His way even without us or despite our best efforts! The grandparents' goal should be to get aligned with Him and

---

ACTION  POINT!

With great gentleness but also fervor, we encourage grandparents to *not* be the ones who lead a grandchild to Christ if the parents are in the position to have that privilege. In our eyes, this decision falls within the parents' responsibility to instruct their children, and your involvement could be an encroachment into their space.

If you think your grandchild is ready, then encourage the parents to take the final step so that they have this tremendously significant spiritual experience.

On the other hand, if the parents are indifferent or opposed, you must tread very carefully to avoid cutting off your access. More importantly, the child might find their ability to grow in Christ would be greatly hampered if the parents are opposed to what happened.

On still another hand, saved children can help their unsaved parents come to know Jesus!

His plan but all of us also need to remember that His grace can create great results out of our mistakes.

To put this point another way, the outcome is not our responsibility, and we should find solace in that situation. However, we can't just throw up our hands and say there's nothing we can or should do in order to fulfill the role that Jesus wants us to experience by helping out as He calls us.

In the way of advice for positive steps to take, we suggest the following ideas to grandparents who find themselves in this situation:

- Pray, pray and pray – for the parents and children to have open hearts, for events to occur in their lives that break down their barriers, for opportunities to share, for your own modeling behavior to speak louder than words, and for victory.

- Give your grandchildren Bibles or Bible storybooks; *Veggie Tales* and other videos can be another way to introduce them to Bible stories and principles.

- When you have openings, read or tell stories from the Bible.

- Describe to your grandchildren how Jesus has been active in your life and in their parents' lives.

- With their parents' permission, take them to church with you and, if it's available, take them to Vacation Bible School or its equivalent; you'll also find that GrandCamp® is a wonderful option.

Here's an important caveat for dealing with this situation. Please, please keep in mind that your witness (and your ability to be with the children) could quickly be lost if you cross some boundary the parents have set. Above all, avoid doing anything that undercuts the parents' position and authority. Backbiting never resolves a problem and is certain to divide the family even more.

You must be patient, faithful, gentle, respectful and, well, patient!

ACTION POINT!

As we just explained, the best starting point for dealing with the situation in which the parents aren't introducing their children to the Gospel is to gently approach them to find out why. You cannot know what to do if you don't know what's causing them to be either silent when it comes to helping their children's faith blossom or, what is much worse, actively denigrating the gospel and deliberately keeping it from them.

In response to whatever you discover, the best thing you can do is explain to the parents how you feel and indicate that you would like the grandchildren to hear more about what you believe. Ask permission to talk to them or, even better, to take them to church with you. Be prepared to be turned down, but keep praying, stand by patiently and don't strike back.

Further, take hope in the fact we just mentioned that it isn't un-known for children to bring their parents to Jesus!

Closing Thoughts

In closing, we hope you have found helpful points for moving ahead in the quest to become "Great Grandparents." We especially hope the Family Trinity has provided insight. Of course, our presentation is incomplete and we've only begun to plumb its depths.

We've also presented unconventional guidance for grandparents because our key point is that *the first role for grandparents is supporting the parents as they instruct their children so they will become successful adults who love God and follow Christ.* Beyond what's here, we hope to explain many other points in subsequent books.

We especially hope that our do's and don'ts about letting go, communicating, helping, reinforcing, spoiling, baby-sitting and gift-giving will help you either keep doing what you've already been doing or to change to something different that will help the parents and children in a new way.

We also hope that you'll share what you learn with other grandparents in your circle of friends and in your family. We have not yet written anything about how to work in concert with your grandchildren's other grandparents, but hope to do so in the future. In the meantime, perhaps you can share with them what you've learned or loan them your copy. Better yet, give them a copy so you can keep yours handy for future reference!

Because we are adoptive parents and grandparents in a multicultural family, we greatly enjoyed writing Chapter 11. Along with our hope for fruit from our advice in the earlier chapters, we deeply desire that this chapter will help you in the context of living within a family that God has built with a non-typical architecture. At the very least, it should allow you to offer encouragement when you interact with other families with that kind of structure.

We confess that Chapter 12 was heartbreaking, first in remembering personal experiences with the death of Paul's mother but also in other deaths that have occurred among our siblings and close friends. We're also broken when we see sad situations in which the parents have taken a different personal and spiritual path from the grandparents. Cavin Harper, our friend and colleague in Christian Grandparenting Network, has devoted much of his life over the last two decades to helping families who are in these situations. If you are among those who face this sadness, we recommend that you read *Courageous Grandparenting*, his very helpful book for dealing with these challenges.

With that point made, we want to thank Cavin and the Network for his vision, the opportunities to serve alongside him, his encouragement, and their assistance in publishing this book.

Our final statement is that we have been privileged to be led by the Holy Spirit to write this book and to enjoy the power of His frequent inspirations when we didn't know what to say or how to say it. We pray that you will let Him, the real author, speak deeply into your hearts as you seek to do God's will as grandparents to your very special grandchildren and coaches for your adult children.

NOTES & PRAYERS

NOTES & PRAYERS

NOTES & PRAYERS

Pass Along Your Legacy of Faith
GRANDCAMP

GrandCamp is truly a transformational experience, and one the best investments you will ever make in the this life. You'll laugh, play, talk, smile and share life together in ways you have not experienced before as you impact their hearts for eternity.

Just want to get your feet wet?

Encourage your church to bring the GrandCamp experience to your congregation through a bond-building Grand Day-Out adventure!

MORE at GrandCamps.org